WILD FL

AND WHERE T(

IN THE CF

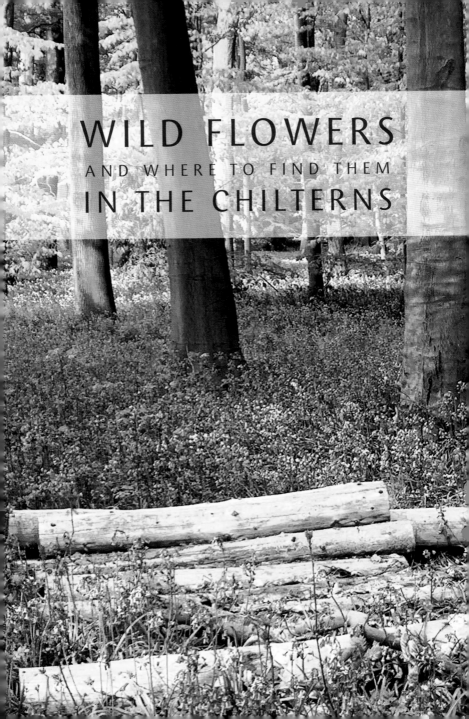

WILD FLOWERS
AND WHERE TO FIND THEM
IN THE CHILTERNS

LAURIE FALLOWS
and GAY FALLOWS
IN CONJUNCTION WITH
THE CHILTERN SOCIETY

FRANCES LINCOLN

A pocket guide to the wild flowers of the Chilterns, their
historical, folk-mythological and medicinal attributes,
with some background essays on related topics ❀ When
and where to find them, their identifying features and
flowering periods ❀ Detailed self-guided walks with
simple maps to facilitate discovery

Also in this series

Wild Flowers and Where to Find Them
in Northern England

Volume 1 **Northern Limestone**
Limestone meadows, pastures and woods

Volume 2 **Waterside Ways**
Streamsides, pond margins, bog and coastal areas

Volume 3 **Acid Uplands**
Mountain, moorland and acid heaths

Frances Lincoln Ltd
4 Torriano Mews, Torriano Avenue, London NW5 2RZ

© 2007 Laurie Fallows and Gay Fallows
Edited and designed by Jane Havell Associates

ISBN 978 0 7112 2780 4

Origination by Chroma Graphics Pte Ltd, Singapore
Printed by South China Printing Co., China
2 4 6 8 9 7 5 3

Half-title page: (top) Common Poppy; (centre) Birdsfoot Trefoil
with a Grizzled Skipper; (bottom) Ribwort Plantain
Title pages: Chiltern bluebell wood
Cover: view of Hartslock Reserve, Oxfordshire

CONTENTS

Acknowledgements   6
The Chiltern Society   7

Introduction   9
  Wild plants and the law   10
  How to use the flower directory   11
  Abbreviations   12
  Botanical terms   13
Geology of the Chilterns   14
Wild Flora of the Chilterns   18

Flower directory   25
Seasonal flowering charts   26
167 of the region's plants   32

Map and map symbols   116
18 beautiful discovery walks   117

Further reading   156
Index of plant names   157

Dedicated to Hazel Fallows – wife and mother –
for her constant love and encouragement

'Look how the wild flowers grow: they do not
work or make clothes for themselves. But not
even King Solomon with all his wealth had
clothes as beautiful as one of these flowers.'
Matthew 6:28 and 29 (Good News Bible)

Acknowledgements

Jane Fallows for producing the maps in the 'Walks' section and the diagrams on
pp 14, 16 and 17.

Angela Bishop, David Henden, Pat Kendell, Clive Ormonde, Hilda Rabbitt and
Alan Turner for walking the routes to catalogue the flora month by month.

Tony Marshall for the section 'Wild Flora of the Chilterns' and expert botanical
advice.

Cic Upcott for the section on The Chiltern Society and her skills in enlisting
ongoing support for the project.

Geoffrey Larminie for the section 'Geology of the Chilterns'.

Ken Poyton, Tony Northwood and members of The Chiltern Society Rights of Way
Group for route suggestions and path clearing.

David Beattie, Brian Colthorpe and members of the Gold Hill Walking Group for
trialling and commenting on all the routes.

Photographers (references are to page numbers):

© Gay Fallows 8, 12, 22, 31, 120, 122, 124, 127, 133, 135, 142, 144, 146, 149,
151, 152

© Laurie Fallows 58 (btm), 62 (btm), 104 (top), 111 (btm), 114 (btm)

© Tony Marshall 19 (both), 23, 67 (btm), 73 (top), 92 (btm), 103 (btm)

© Clive Ormonde: cover, 1 (all), 21, 24–25, 32–58 (top), 59–62 (top), 63–67
(top), 68–72, 73 (btm)–80 (top), 81–88, 89 (btm)–92 (top), 93–103 (top),
104 (btm)–111 (top), 112–114 (top), 115

© Ken Poyton 80 (btm), 89 (top)

© Alan Turner Photography 2–3, 118

The **Chiltern** Society

We care for the Chilterns

The Chilterns are a long range of chalk hills and grasslands, covering 1,700 sq km/ 650 square miles to the north west of London – in Oxfordshire, Buckinghamshire, Hertfordshire and Bedfordshire – and encompassing the Chilterns AONB, Area of Outstanding Natural Beauty (about 850 sq km/325 square miles). The region is threaded with deep valleys and streams, as well as major transport routes and waterways. Large towns and small, delightful villages are set in beautiful countryside, attracting thousands of walkers and visitors all year round.

The Chiltern Society, founded in 1965, is a large environmental organisation, with some 7,500 members. The Society's major objective – 'Caring for the Chilterns' – is undertaken by a large number of members in many practical ways, including maintaining, walking and mapping 3,700 km/2,300 miles of linked paths and bridleways; watching over water resources, heritage buildings and all aspects of planning, and undertaking many conservation projects. The Society owns a woodland nature reserve (Walk 9), Ewelme watercress beds and a windmill (seen from Walk 15), and is directly responsible for setting up other projects, such as the Chiltern Open Air Museum. The Society's broad activities and interests, including a Primary Schools Education Project, a Farming Liaison Group, a Photographic Group and a Cycling Group, are reflected and reported in its quarterly magazine *Chiltern News*.

The Society works closely with the Chilterns (AONB) Conservation Board, the Council for the Protection of Rural England, the National Trust and other organisations, both large and small. All County, District, Parish and Town Councils are in membership, the smaller councils benefiting from the help given to maintain footpaths by the experienced Path Maintenance Volunteers. There is also close cooperation with the many amenity groups, and meetings of the Civic Trust's Association of North Thames Amenity Societies are regularly attended.

A small team of enthusiastic Chiltern Society volunteers has made an invaluable contribution to *Wild Flowers and Where to Find Them in the Chilterns* by monitoring the flowers each month, taking the photographs and writing the introductory essays.

To find out more about The Chiltern Society, visit www.chilternsociety.org.uk or telephone the Society's office in Chesham on 01494 771250.

INTRODUCTION

As more and more people take quiet recreation in country walks, the need for simple, descriptive, illustrated guides to wild flowers has increased. Existing flower guides have a number of drawbacks for beginners. They often rely on a knowledge of botanical terms, and do not indicate where particular species may be found. The popular appeal of the three volumes *Wild Flowers and Where to Find Them in Northern England* (Frances Lincoln, 2004) encouraged us to make similar information available for the Chilterns to those who enjoy a good walk and appreciate the contribution of the flowers to the general beauty of the countryside. The expertise and enthusiasm of several members of The Chiltern Society have been invaluable in the production of this volume.

The plants covered in this book are not usually specific to the region, but can be found in other regions with similar soils and climates throughout the rest of Britain. Space does not permit an exhaustive list of species found in the Chilterns, and so very well-known flowers have been omitted (such as Buttercup, Clover, Daisy, Dandelion, Dog Rose, Forget-me-not, Foxglove, Snowdrop and the more common thistles), as have less significant ones (such as Chickweed, Cleavers) and those easily confused (many Crucifers, Umbellifers and the Hawkish complex). A general pocket guide to wild flowers will fill any gaps for the enthusiast (for suggestions see Further Reading).

Descriptions are stated in the simplest terms, and do not require any knowledge of the technical vocabulary of botanists. Read in association with the colour photographs, they should prevent confusion and make for certain identification. The walks are located in the Greater Chilterns area, which includes Oxfordshire, Buckinghamshire, Hertfordshire and Bedfordshire.

Opposite: lane near Bix Bottom leading to the Warburg BBOWT Reserve (see Walk 6).

They feature sections of several long-distance paths, including The Chiltern Way, The Icknield Way (axe symbol), and The Ridgeway National Trail (acorn symbol). Many walks pass through or very close to nature reserves. The straightforward instructions are illustrated by specially drawn, simple maps, with a note of the relevant Ordnance Survey maps and Chiltern Society footpath maps for those who want further cartographical information. Distances are given in kilometres and miles, and average walk times are shown. While some of the walks are longer than others, the maps often show how these may be shortened.

RESPECT FOR HABITATS

All the plants featured in this book have been recorded within two metres of public or permissive footpaths. If the walk guides are followed, there is no risk of trespass. Where reserves allow Open Access, this is mentioned. Remember to tread carefully and avoid trampling plants when looking at or photographing them, especially rare species.

Common flowers may be picked to aid identification, but plants must never be uprooted. Apart from being illegal (see box, below), removing them detracts from the natural environment.

WILD PLANTS AND THE LAW

All plants growing in the wild and their habitats are protected by the Wildlife and Countryside Act, 1981. Section 13 states: 'It is an offence for anyone to intentionally pick, uproot or destroy any wild plant on schedule 8,' which includes, among others, Bluebells. European legislation embodied in Conservation (Natural Habitats, etc.) Regulations 1994 adds further plants. Section 13 (1)(b) of the 1981 Act states: 'It is an offence for any unauthorised person to intentionally uproot any wild plant,' – i.e., whether it is protected or not. Dealing in wild plants is forbidden under Section 13 (2) (9a), which makes it an offence to 'sell, offer or expose for sale or possess or transport for the purpose of sale, or advertisement of intent to sell, any live or dead wild plant (or any part of or anything derived from such a plant) on schedule 8.'

Section 4 (3) of the Theft Act 1968 states that the picking of wild flowers, fruit or fungi for reward is considered to be theft. Uprooting a whole plant may also be considered theft.

CONSUMPTION

The herbal uses described in this guide are for general interest only. Plants and plant extracts must not be applied to the skin or taken internally without reference to a qualified herbalist or at least an up-to-date herbal. Very careful identification is essential before any kind of experiment. Even in recent times, people have died through incorrect identification of plants – for example, by confusing Foxglove leaves with Comfrey. Identification should be by examining the whole plant, not just the flower or the leaf alone, since there are many superficial similarities.

HOW TO USE THE FLOWER DIRECTORY

The plants are grouped according to the main colours of their flowers. However, many may be present in different colours – for example, Milkwort varies from blue or pink to white, and Comfrey from pale cream to purple. Flower colour should be only one factor in identifying a species.

FLOWERING CHARTS

The Directory begins with colour charts, showing the months in which the plants may be seen in flower. Colours can vary considerably, even within species, so this should be taken as only a rough guide to aid identification. For simplification, and because colour is often subjective, the charts include some flowers that fit only marginally into the given colour categories.

While the charts are a general guide to flowering times, individual specimens may flower outside these months. This may be due to peculiar local conditions or global weather changes or may be because some species flower in profusion for a month or two and then produce a second flush later in the year. A few, such as White Dead-nettle, may be seen virtually all the year round.

PHOTOGRAPHS

Species are illustrated by a colour photograph, showing the general appearance of the plant, and the shape and relative size of its leaves and flowers. Please note that the scale of the individual photographs is not consistent.

Summer pasture.

NAMES

The main English name is given first, then any other names in common use. Vernacular names can be confusing. In different parts of the country, a single flower can have many different names – Lords-and-Ladies, for example, has at least ninety recorded local names. The name Thunderflower is used for both Wood Anemone and Wood Crane's-bill; Aaron's Rod for Agrimony and Great Mullein. Latin names are therefore also given to aid

ABBREVIATIONS

AS	Anglo-Saxon
Celt	Celtic
Fr	French
Ger	German
Gk	Greek
L	Latin
OE	Old English
OFr	Old French
ON	Old Norse

precise identification. Wherever possible, the origin and explanation of both Latin and common names are expounded.

HEIGHT AND FLOWERING MONTHS

When identifying a plant, do not refer just to the photograph, but also to the height in the written description.

DESCRIPTION

The account of general characteristics is followed by particulars of where the plant grows, and an indication of its place in folklore and in folk and contemporary medicine.

BOTANICAL TERMS

Every effort has been made to keep plant descriptions as simple as possible, but a few botanical terms are unavoidable.

alternate arranged alternately up the stem

annual completing a full life cycle in one year

anthers cases on top of stamens that contain pollen

basal just above ground level at the foot of the stem

biennial forming a rosette of basal leaves the first year; raising a stem, flowering and dying in the second year

bract small, leaf-like organ on flower stem

calyx sepals at flower base, often joined in a cup or tube

deciduous shedding leaves in the autumn

floret individual flower in a tight arrangement, as in Daisy

labiate in two parts, like lips

lanceolate lance-shaped

leaflet one division of a compound leaf

lobed divided into sections

node place on stem where leaves arise

ovary the seed container below the style

perennial going on year after year with incremental vegetative increase

persistent leaves overwinter on plant

petals inner leaves, often highly coloured, of flower heads

pinnate divided into leaflets either side of stalk

raceme flower spike

rhizome swollen underground root that feeds the plant

sepals outer leaves of flower buds and holders of flower

stamens male pollen-bearing organs

stigma top of the style that receives the pollen

stipules small leaf-like appendages at the base of leaf stalks

stolons creeping stems that produce new plant stems at intervals

style tube or stalk between stigma and ovary

trefoil with three leaflets, as in Clover

tubers swollen underground organs with plant food

wintergreen retaining old leaves over winter

IDENTIFICATION TIPS

When trying to identify a plant you do not know, it is important to consider all its features – particularly the shape of both flower and leaves, whether or not parts are hairy, whether it is growing in dry or wet conditions, in sun or in shade, and whether it is shunned or devoured by livestock. Consider its situation in relation to the type of ground it is growing in and its association with other plant life. Climate and altitude can also cause considerable variation. The Walks section gives further information about when and where to locate certain species.

A small hand lens of 10× magnification is very helpful in identification, and also reveals the hidden beauties of diminutive species.

GEOLOGY OF THE CHILTERNS

The central and southern Chilterns are a fine example of the topographic form called a cuesta. Defined as an asymmetrical ridge, a cuesta is the product of millennia of differential erosion of gently dipping strata. On one side, the slope of the topography is coincident with the dip of the resistant strata forming the main mass of the cuesta (Cretaceous chalk in the Chilterns), and on the other, the strata are truncated at a high angle to form a short, steep scarp. The Chiltern escarpment trends SE/NW and dies out NE of Hitchin, giving way to low hills and an irregular rolling topography. This transition marks the southern limit of glaciation in the Chilterns, and the landscape NE of Hitchin is the product of an over-riding ice sheet which lowered the topography by at least 100 metres.

The Cretaceous age chalk of the scarp and dip slope comprises the main mass of the Chilterns cuesta and the unique qualities of the English chalk-lands are perfectly encapsulated in this quotation from Richard Fortey's *The Hidden Landscape*: 'Chalk: commonplace stuff at first glance, but chalk is special. In no other part of the geological record are the connections

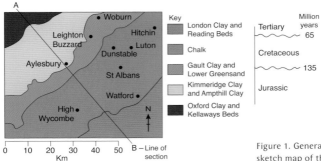

Figure 1. Generalised geological sketch map of the Chilterns.

between landscape, flora, farming, history and the rocks beneath so clear as in the case of chalk.'

Though pre-eminent, there is more to the Chilterns than the chalk, and what follows is a very brief and highly selective outline of salient elements of the geology of the region (see Figures 1, 2 and 3).

100 million years ago
GAULT: a marine deposit (full of marine fossils), mainly clay forming the low-lying land at the base of the chalk escarpment (part of the Vale of Aylesbury) and LOWER GREENSAND: thin, discontinuous sand and sandy mudstone. *Period of marked deepening of the sea and virtual cessation of any terrestrial sediment input.*

60–100 million years ago
CHALK: deposited in a warm sea 300+ metres deep during the Cretaceous period; no nearby land (? desert shores); almost pure calcium carbonate without any terrigenous sediment contamination. Almost entirely composed of fossils, mainly coccoliths (calcite plates secreted by microscopic, planktonic, unicellular marine algae) and foraminifera (minute, single-celled planktonic protozoans). FLINT: a form of silica (SiO_2) occurring as discrete nodules or in bands which closely follow the bedding. It too is organic, formed from the skeletal elements of marine sponges, single-celled radiolarians and diatoms. *Major earth movements at the end of the Cretaceous resulted in a fall in sea level and most of Britain emerged as land with a sub-tropical climate.*

57–60 million years ago
LAMBETH GROUP (including READING BEDS): c. 15 metres of riverine and shallow marine coastal sediments comprising sand, pebbles and clay. Represented in the Chilterns by scattered sarsens (Aston Rowant) and pudding stones (The Lee, Chesham Bois) – these rocks are very hard and are the result of silica-rich water percolating through and cementing the sediments. *Further earth movements and tilting of the land.*

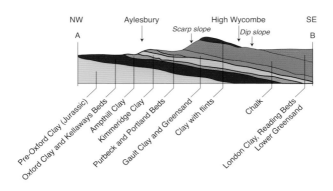

Figure 2. Diagrammatic section of the line A–B in Figure 1 (not to scale).

51–57 million years ago

LONDON CLAY: c. 100 metres of dark, bluish-grey clay deposited in a shallow sub-tropical sea which encroached on the land. Conditions were sub-tropical with a swampy coastal plain and rainforest bordering the sea. *Major earth movements c. 40 million years ago raised the land and over millions of years the pre-existing deposits were weathered and eroded.*

2–3 million years ago

QUATERNARY: in contrast to the above (which are rock terms), the Quaternary is a time period marked by considerable global climatic instability. Deposits in the Chilterns comprise river gravels, clay-with-flints, plateau drift, and over a third of the chalk is covered by clay-with-flints (a product of frost and water action on pre-existing rocks under a periglacial regime). Ice dominated Britain with a cyclical series of advances and retreats, and in one advance (known as the Anglian advance) c. 300,000 years ago, an ice sheet c. 1,000 metres thick overrode the northern end of the Chilterns from the north-east. Finally, there are very large deposits of sand and gravel to the south (Thames Valley terraces), and to the east and southeast (St Albans – course of the proto-Thames before diversion by the Anglian ice).

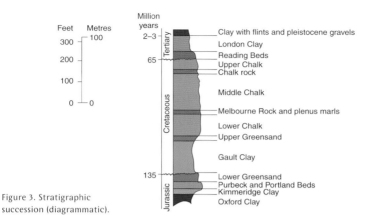

Figure 3. Stratigraphic succession (diagrammatic).

SOILS

The chalk, clay-with-flints, and sands and gravels are the dominant elements of the substrata influencing vegetation, but over large areas the connections have become blurred as a consequence of man's activities over the millennia. Outcrops are scattered and in places, it is the plants that provide the clues to the type of underlying rock – for example, Traveller's-joy (Wild Clematis) is the most 'lime-loving' or 'lime-sensitive' plant of all.

Chalk pits are very common in the Chilterns and were dug to get lime to spread on the thin, very acidic, leached soils associated with the clay-with-flints (e.g. the strongly acidic, infertile soils of the Burnham plateau). Where chalk pits escaped disturbance by agriculture they are often important refuges for species which have declined as a result of cultivation.

Down the dip slope of the Chilterns, towards London, the Lambeth Group and the London Clay are rarely seen. Over time they have become inextricably mixed with glacial, periglacial and riverine deposits and the result is a wide range of clays, silts, sands, gravels and brick-earths.

WILD FLORA OF THE CHILTERNS

Wild flowers vary considerably across Britain with the climate, from the warm south to the cold north, from the dry east to the damp west, from the sheltered lowlands to the exposed uplands. The Chilterns, however, combine features of all these. In the south of the country but far from the south coast, they lack the Mediterranean-type plants that survive on the latter, and their elevation (however modest) makes for a cooler climate than the surrounding lowlands. Somewhat east of centre, they still share some plants with the west, like the splendid displays of Bluebells more typical of the Atlantic seaboard, and Primroses one associates particularly with Devon lanes, although deficient in the variety of ferns and mosses those wetter regions offer.

The geology is important, too. The chalk soils are poor for crops that need plenty of nitrogen and phosphorus, but they allow specially adapted plants to survive where competition from more vigorous ones is reduced. As a result, chalk hills support a wider variety of flowers than almost any other region, and the bonus is that most of them are very pretty too! A rich turf of Clustered Bellflower, Basil Thyme (*Clinopodium acinos*), Long-stalked Crane's-bill (*Geranium columbinum*), Milkwort, Quaking-grass (*Briza media*), Bee Orchid and Yellow-wort is a sight to be treasured. The clays that cap the hills vary locally in chemical composition, according to the circumstances of their deposition, from somewhat alkaline to very acid, so that the plants they support vary markedly; they include pockets of grass-heath where one gets Heather (*Calluna vulgaris*), Tormentil, Gorse (*Ulex europaeus*) and Harebell. Moorend Common is a prime example of Chiltern heath, with Petty Whin (*Genista anglica*), and both Heath Spotted and Southern Marsh Orchids (which may hybridise to confuse the botanist). The glory of the

Fringed Gentian.

Bird's-nest Orchid.

Chilterns is that, in the course of a single walk, one may traverse this whole variety of habitats and different communities of flowers. And winding around the chalk hills is a narrow band of hard limestone-like chalk-rock, separating the Middle Chalk from the flintier Upper Chalk, which provides special conditions where some of the rarest flowers grow, such as Common Rock-rose and Fringed Gentian (*Gentianella ciliata*).

Apart from the climate and the geology, the main influence on the flora of the Chilterns is man-management. The former heathy commons are now rare because these were infertile areas, of little use for either agri- or sylviculture, and so were the first to be built upon during the population expansions of the Industrial Revolution and later. The steep upper slopes of the chalk valleys were difficult to plough, and so these were largely left to woodland, providing the famous beech hangers that are tough for walkers, but beautiful in spring and autumn, with some of our rarer and secretive flowers, such as Yellow Bird's-nest (*Monotropa hypotitys*) and Bird's-nest Orchid

(*Neottia nidus-avis*). The clay tops, stiff and stony to work, were often left to woodland where different species are found, such as Early Dog-violet, Violet Helleborine, trees such as Hornbeam (*Carpinus betulus*) and Wild Service (*Sorbus torminalis*), and various uncommon grasses. These woods became economically important in the eighteenth, nineteenth and early twentieth centuries for the provision of beech for the furniture industry in towns such as High Wycombe. Many were clear-felled to monocultures of beech trees which are now a feature of the Chiltern landscape, but they were not always so: the old woods contained a wide variety of trees – oak and ash, whitebeam and yew, birch and rowan – of which beech was only a minor component.

Sheep were traditionally pastured on the chalk hills and they kept the turf short, suitable for many of the special orchids and other downland flowers. Many of these pastures, and their plants, have disappeared with the demise of commercial sheep-farming and now survive largely in conservation areas. Even ploughed land had its special suite of flowers, ingenious annuals that could grow among the corn, flower and seed before the crop was cut, leaving their seeds in the soil for future years. With modern chemical fertilisers and weed-killers these plants have become some of the rarest in the area – Venus's-looking-glass (*Legousia hybrida*), Small Toadflax (*Chaenorhinum minus*), Fluellens, Cornsalads (*Valerianella* spp) and Fumitories. Only on field margins and in specially protected areas, such as organic farms, can these still be found. Unfertilised old hay-meadows, grazed through winter, have largely disappeared, but they have a special flora, even on the clays, of Cowslip, Devil's-bit Scabious, Betony, Pignut and Grass Vetchling.

The difficulty of the soils and the topography gave Chiltern farming a special character – mixed arable and pasture, orchards and ponds, small fields separated by hedgerows that often date back to the first settlements in Anglo-Saxon times, and it was this farming that shaped the varied and beautiful landscape we see today. In the modern economy, however, this type of farming is under threat, and with it the landscape, its plants and animals. Nature reserves are crucial but not sufficient – one must pin one's hopes now on government support for schemes such as Environmental Stewardship that provide farmers with some compensation for continuing traditional methods that conserve the wider environment.

Chalk grassland flowers, Hartslock, Oxfordshire.

The tapestry of different habitats resulting from man's use of the land, the topography of rounded hills and steep valleys, and the underlying geology are what make the Chilterns rich country for the botanist. There are few plants that are specific to the area – its chalk grassland flowers, for instance, are generally shared with other downlands south of the Thames – but a few that are confined, or almost so, to the Chilterns, are worthy of special mention here.

Of these fourteen, half are associated with short chalk grass turf, needing grazing to keep down coarse grasses and scrub, whether (as traditionally) by sheep, or (more commonly nowadays) by rabbits, roe-deer and muntjac. Unfortunately, the latter tend to eat off the flowers too, and many of the plants only survive by the intervention of conservationists. This particularly applies to the Military and Monkey Orchids. The first grows at the southern tip of the Chilterns at Hartslock NR, one of only two extant sites in the

Leafy bridleway near West Wycombe (see Walk 9).

country, rescued after it was illegally ploughed up. The second has three of its current sites in the Chilterns, the main one at Homefield Wood NR. That striking anemone Pasque Flower particularly likes the dry banks of ancient earthworks, but is very much declining, as is the large-flowered Eyebright (*Euphrasia pseudokerneri*). A much less striking umbellifer, Moon Carrot (*Seseli libanotis*), grows at three sites, all SSSIs, at the north end of the Chilterns and the extension of the same chalk ridge as far as Cambridge. The Chilterns' only eponymous flower, the Chiltern Gentian, on the other hand, can still be found in quantity at a good many sites, and has been voted as the county flower of Buckinghamshire. There are concerns about it hybridising with its near relative the Autumn Gentian, which is also widespread. Another relative, the delicate blue Fringed Gentian, by contrast, barely survives in the central Chilterns at its only site in the country, right beside the busiest footpath in the area, although it appears to have survived here for over a hundred years at very low frequency. The difficulty of finding it is increased by the fact that it only flowers briefly in full sunshine quite unpredictably anywhere between August and October!

Two other special plants are sometimes found in chalk grassland, although they like barer or disturbed areas, including arable land. They are Wild Candytuft, which largely survives on rabbit scrapes (e.g. at Aston Rowant NNR) and Great Pignut (*Bunium bulbocastanum*), which has a similar distribution to its relation, Moon Carrot.

Four plants are associated with the chalk beechwoods. Yellow Bird's-nest is decreasing and must be sought in the darkest areas, being a saprophyte which lives off decaying vegetable remains, and having no green leaves to manufacture chlorophyll. In similar places, and also without green parts, the Ghost Orchid (*Epipogium aphyllum*) was once seen in various places in the Henley region, but not since 1986. The Red Helleborine (*Cephalanthera rubra*) has one site in a nature reserve in the central Chilterns, and only two elsewhere in the country, and grows only in small numbers. The Coralroot, however, a close relative of the common Cuckooflower, still grows plentifully in a few woods in the High Wycombe–Beaconsfield region, where it spreads by vegetative 'bulbils' that grow at the base of its leaves and drop to the ground, as well as by seed.

Red Helleborine.

Lastly, there is a strange plant which grows only on bare acid mud beside ponds that are regularly trampled by stock. The Starfruit (*Damasonium alisma*) has small three-petalled white flowers, but these develop into clusters of enlarged fruits that spread like a star. It has been brought back from the brink of extinction at Gerrards Cross Common by the efforts of conservationists led by Buckinghamshire County Council's Andy McVeigh. It used to be frequent before the decline in the use of farm ponds for watering cows.

Primroses, Homefield Wood, Buckinghamshire.

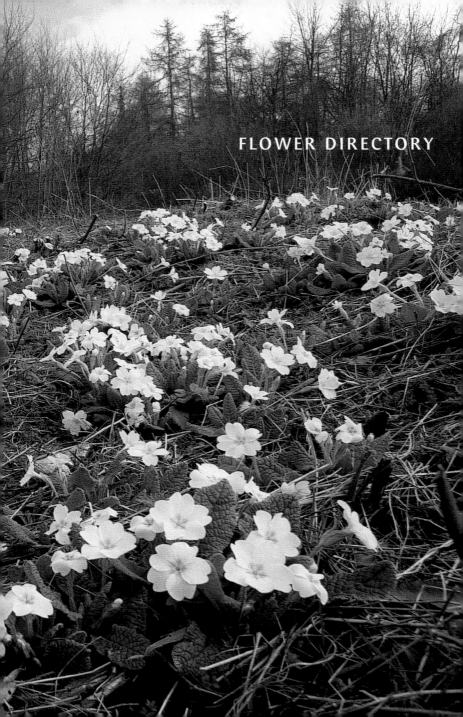

PLANTS IN FLOWER	Jan	Feb	Mar	Apr	May	June	July	Aug	Sep	Oct	Nov	Dec
Agrimony												
Archangel, Yellow												
Avens, Wood												
Bedstraw, Lady's												
Bird's-foot-trefoil												
Celandine, Lesser												
Cinquefoil, Creeping												
Coltsfoot												
Cowslip												
Fleabane, Common												
Fluellen, Round-leaved												
Goat's-beard												
Iris, Yellow												
Marsh-marigold												
Melilot, Ribbed												
Mignonette, Wild												
Mullein, Dark												
Nipplewort												
Parsnip, Wild												
Pimpernel, Yellow												
Pineappleweed												
Ploughman's-spikenard												
Primrose												
Ragwort, Common												
Rock-rose, Common												
St John's-wort												
Silverweed												
Sow-thistle, Perennial												
Thistle, Carline												
Toadflax, Common												
Tormentil												
Vetchling, Meadow												
Yellow-rattle												
Yellow-wort												

PLANTS IN FLOWER	Jan	Feb	Mar	Apr	May	June	July	Aug	Sep	Oct	Nov	Dec
Anemone, Wood												
Angelica, Wild												
Bedstraw, Hedge												
Bindweed, Field												
Bryony, White												
Campion, Bladder												
Campion, White												
Candytuft, Wild												
Carrot, Wild												
Catmint, Wild												
Dead-nettle, White												
Dropwort												
Enchanter's-nightshade												
Eyebright												
Feverfew												
Flax, Fairy												
Hemlock												
Hogweed												
Mayweed, Scentless												
Meadowsweet												
Mustard, Garlic												
Orchid, Greater Butterfly												
Pansy, Field												
Parsley, Cow												
Parsley, Fool's												
Parsley, Hedge												
Pignut												
Ramsons												
Sanicle												
Sneezewort												
Snowflake, Summer												
Squinancywort												
Star-of-Bethlehem												
Stitchwort, Greater												
Strawberry, Wild												
Traveller's-joy												
Water-crowfoot, Chalkstream												
Water-dropwort, Hemlock												
Water-cress												
Woodruff												
Wood-sorrel												
Yarrow												

PLANTS IN FLOWER	Jan	Feb	Mar	Apr	May	June	July	Aug	Sep	Oct	Nov	Dec
Basil, Wild						X	X	X		X		
Betony						X	X	X	X			
Bittersweet						X	X	X	X			
Comfrey, Common					X	X	X	X	X			
Dead-nettle, Red			X		X	X	X	X	X	X	X	X
Gentian, Autumn								X	X	X		
Gentian, Chiltern								X	X			
Goat's-rue						X	X	X				
Ground-ivy			X	X	X	X	X					
Horehound, Black						X	X	X	X			
Hound's-tongue					X	X	X	X				
Iris, Stinking						X	X	X				
Knapweed, Common						X	X	X	X			
Knapweed, Greater						X	X	X	X			
Lucerne						X	X	X	X	X		
Madder, Field					X	X	X	X	X			
Marjoram							X	X	X			
Mint, Water							X	X	X	X		
Orchid, Common Spotted					X	X	X	X				
Orchid, Southern Marsh					X	X	X	X				
Pasque Flower				X	X							
Purple-loosestrife						X	X	X	X			
Scabious, Devil's-bit						X	X	X	X			
Scabious, Field						X	X	X	X	X		
Selfheal						X	X	X	X	X		
Teasel, Wild							X	X	X			
Thistle, Dwarf							X	X	X			
Thistle, Musk						X	X	X	X			
Thyme, Wild					X	X	X	X	X			
Toadflax, Pale						X	X	X	X	X		
Vervain						X	X	X	X	X		
Vetch, Bush					X	X	X	X	X	X		
Vetch, Common					X	X	X	X	X			
Vetch, Tufted					X	X	X	X				
Violet, Early Dog			X	X	X							
Violet, Sweet		X	X	X	X							
Woundwort, Hedge						X	X	X	X	X		
Woundwort, Marsh						X	X	X	X	X		

PLANTS IN FLOWER	Jan	Feb	Mar	Apr	May	June	July	Aug	Sep	Oct	Nov	Dec
Balsam, Himalayan							■	■	■			
Bartsia, Red						■	■	■	■	■		
Campion, Red			■	■	■	■	■	■	■	■		
Centaury, Common						■	■	■	■			
Coralroot				■	■	■						
Crane's-bill, Cut-leaved					■	■	■	■	■			
Crane's-bill, Dove's-foot				■	■	■	■	■	■			
Crane's-bill, Hedgerow					■	■	■	■	■			
Cuckooflower			■	■	■	■						
Fumitory				■	■	■	■	■	■	■		
Hemp-agrimony							■	■	■			
Herb-Robert				■	■	■	■	■	■	■		
Mallow, Common						■	■	■	■			
Musk-mallow						■	■	■				
Orchid, Bee						■	■					
Orchid, Fragrant						■	■	■				
Orchid, Lady					■	■						
Orchid, Military					■	■						
Orchid, Monkey					■	■						
Orchid, Pyramidal						■	■	■				
Ragged-Robin					■	■	■					
Restharrow						■	■	■	■			
Valerian, Common						■	■	■	■			
Willowherb, Great						■	■	■	■			
Willowherb, Rosebay							■	■	■			

PLANTS IN FLOWER	Jan	Feb	Mar	Apr	May	June	July	Aug	Sep	Oct	Nov	Dec
Balsam, Orange							■	■	■			
Burnet, Salad					■	■	■	■				
Pimpernel, Scarlet					■	■	■	■	■	■		
Vetchling, Grass					■	■	■					

PLANTS IN FLOWER	Jan	Feb	Mar	Apr	May	June	July	Aug	Sep	Oct	Nov	Dec
Alkanet, Green			■	■	■	■	■					
Bellflower, Clustered						■	■	■	■			
Bellflower, Nettle-leaved						■	■	■	■	■		
Bluebell				■	■	■						
Borage					■	■	■	■	■			
Brooklime					■	■	■	■	■			
Bugle				■	■	■	■					
Chicory							■	■	■	■		
Harebell							■	■	■	■		
Milkwort, Common					■	■	■	■	■			
Speedwell, Common Field	■	■	■	■	■	■	■	■	■	■	■	■
Speedwell, Germander			■	■	■	■	■	■				
Speedwell, Ivy-leaved		■	■	■	■							
Speedwell, Thyme-leaved			■	■	■	■	■	■	■			
Speedwell, Wood				■	■	■	■					
Viper's-bugloss						■	■	■	■			

PLANTS IN FLOWER	Jan	Feb	Mar	Apr	May	June	July	Aug	Sep	Oct	Nov	Dec
Helleborine, Violet							■	■				
Lords-and-Ladies				■	■							
Mercury, Dog's		■	■	■	■							
Moschatel				■	■							
Orchid, Frog						■	■	■				
Plantain, Hoary					■	■	■					
Spurge, Wood			■	■	■							
Twayblade, Common					■	■	■					

Opposite: Chicory growing along a footpath near Middle Assendon (near Walk 6).

AGRIMONY

FAIRY'S ROD, FAIRY WAND, AARON'S ROD,
CHURCH STEEPLES, STICKLEWORT

Height 30–60 cm/12–24 in 🌸 June–September

Agrimonia eupatoria
Gk *argemos*, white speck on the eye (which
agrimony was believed to cure); Eupatoria
after Mithridates Eupator, King of Pontus, who
introduced it as a medicine and was reputed to
be immune to poisons

Faintly perfumed perennial. Woody root. Erect
round and roughish stems, seldom branched.
Pinnate leaves like ash, 3–6 main leaflets with
smaller ones between, downy below, sharply
toothed. Small yellow flowers make slim spike,
5-petalled, widely spaced. Fruits are small oval
burs, hooked and furrowed. Staunches
bleeding, encourages blood clotting. Wide
variety of medicinal uses. Taken in wine
against snake bites. Yields a yellow dye.

ARCHANGEL, YELLOW

WEASEL SNOUT, YELLOW DEAD-NETTLE

Height 20–60 cm/8–24 in 🌸 April–June

Lamiastrum galeobdolon
L *lamiastrum*, resembling Lamium, the genus
name for dead-nettle, possibly from Gk *laimos*,
throat (referring to the shape of the flowers)
Gk *galee*, weasel; Gk *bdolos*, disagreeable odour
(hence 'smells like a weasel')
Archangel after Archangel Michael on whose
day (29 Sep) dead-nettles are still in flower

A hairy perennial with long creeping stolons
that create large patches in woods and
waysides. Hairy upright square stems bear
opposite pairs of pointed-oval, deeply toothed
leaves with many narrow bracts in spaced-out
whorls. Unstalked yellow flowers crowd into
leaf axils: erect hooded upper lip, lower lip 3-
lobed with brown honey-guides. Seeds are
brown nutlets. Strong-smelling. Believed to
protect people from evil spirits and spells, and
cattle from elf-shot, a magic affliction.
Culpeper recommended it for sores and ulcers.

AVENS, WOOD

HERB BENNET, GOLDY STAR, CLOVE-ROOT,
THE HERB OF ST BENEDICT

Height 30–60 cm/12–24 in ❀ May–September

Geum urbanum
L *geum* from Gk *geno*, to yield an agreeable
fragrance; L *urbanum*, related to towns

A perennial plant with a stout woody rhizome.
Leaves at base pinnate, with 2–5 pairs of
unequal leaflets, the terminal one largest.
Stem leaves longer, almost trefoil. All leaves
toothed. Upright small yellow flowers on
individual stems with long green sepals
interspacing petals. Fruits in round cluster like
a bur, each seed hooked for animal dispersal.
Roots have a delicate clove-like aroma used to
repel moths and flies, and to flavour ale and
Benedictine liqueur. Infusion taken against
diarrhoea, stomach and liver upsets and as a
mouthwash. Highly recommended by
Culpeper. In bath water, it heals cuts and piles.

BEDSTRAW, LADY'S

CHEESE RENNET, MAIDEN'S HAIR

Height 15–60 cm/6–24 in ❀ June–September

Galium verum
Gk *gala*, milk; L *verum*, true

A sprawling perennial with rounded stems
having 4 lines of hairs. Dark green shiny
leaves, hairy below in whorls of 8 to 12 with
down-facing margins. Golden flowers in a
fluffy oval bunch smelling of honey. Small
green fruits turn black when ripe. In medieval
times it was reputed that Mary lay on this herb
because the donkeys had eaten all the hay;
hence it was believed to bring safe and easy
childbirth. When dry it smells of new-mown
hay. Once used to stuff mattresses, it was
believed to deter fleas. Herbal medicinal uses
against dropsy, kidney and bladder disorders,
and stomach upsets. External use for skin
infections, slow-healing cuts and grazes.
Flowers used to curdle milk in cheese making.
Leaves give yellow dye, roots red.

BIRD'S-FOOT-TREFOIL, COMMON

BACON AND EGGS, GOD ALMIGHTY'S THUMB
AND FINGER (up to 70 UK local names)

Height 10–40 cm/4–16 in ✿ May–September

Lotus corniculatus
Gk *lotos*, name of various leguminous plants
L *corniculatus*, horned

A sprawling perennial with solid stems rising
from a woody rootstock. Shamrock-like leaves
with 2 stipules below. Up to 7 flowers form a
flat circular head above a longish stalk. Pea-
like flowers yellow, often with red streaks,
have a beaked keel. The fruits are in straight
pods that twist as they open to release their
seeds, making the fruit head appear like a
bird's foot. Usually found in short grass or
roadside verges. One of its local names was No
Blame: Irish children used to carry it to school
to help them avoid punishment.

CELANDINE, LESSER

PILEWORT, FOALFOOT, SPRING MESSENGER,
GOLDEN GUINEA

Height 6–15 cm/2.5–6 in ✿ March–May

Ranunculus ficaria
L *rana*, frog (allusion to preference for damp
locations); L *ficaria*, fig-like (shape of tubers)
Celandine comes from Gk *khelidon*, swallow, a
bird believed to use the flowers to improve the
sight of its chicks

A low hairless perennial with knobbly
tuberous roots like piles. Fleshy dark green
leaves, long-stalked, heart-shaped, sometimes
with dark blotches. Solitary flowers with 8–12
glossy yellow petals that close in dull weather.
Fruits in a small round cluster. Formerly the
leaves were used medicinally against piles and
scurvy. Cosmetic lotion made from Celandine
cleanses skin, closes pores and removes
wrinkles. Use leaves sparingly in salads or
sandwiches; leaves, stalks and buds as spinach;
buds can be preserved like capers.

CINQUEFOIL, CREEPING

Height 5–10 cm/2–4 in ❀ June–September

Potentilla reptans
L *potentilla*, quite powerful (as a medicinal
herb); L *reptans*, creeping

A perennial rising from a stout stock of
creeping stems (up to 100 cm/40 in) that root
at nodes. Toothed leaves are divided into 5 or
7 leaflets (like Horse Chestnut) on long
stalks. Single 5-petalled flowers on long slim
stalks from leaf nodes. Yellow petals notched.
Fruit a dry achene (like a small nut).
Dioscorides said this plant, called Five Fingers,
was good against malaria, based on its magical
powers, but Gerard dismissed this as 'foolish'.
Astringent roots and leaves used as a febrifuge,
mouthwash, and against haemorrhages and
dysentery, also for bathing cuts and for piles.
Roots once used for tanning. In Scotland it
was hung in doorways to deter witches.

COLT'S-FOOT

COUGHWORT, COLDWORT, CLEATS, FOAL-
FOOT, HORSE HOOF, ASSES FOOT, BULL FOOT

Height 3–17 cm/1.5–7 in ❀ February–April

Tussilago farfara
L *tussilago*, dispeller of coughs (L *tussis*, cough)
? *farfara*, extremely mealy (etymology
uncertain)

A perennial rising from an underground
rhizome, flowers before leaves. Yellow daisy-
like flowers borne on erect, purplish, scaly
stem. After flowering, mealy white heart-
shaped basal leaves with crinkled edges
appear. Umbrella-type leaves, upper parts
shiny, felted white below. The apothecaries'
shop-sign. Used for coughs and colds, asthma,
pleurisy, bites, ulcers, swellings and burns.
Dried leaves used as snuff and 'tobacco',
especially for asthmatics. Leaves dipped in
saltpetre used as tinder. Makes wine called
'Clayt', and a beer called 'Cleats'. Use young
leaves, buds and flowers for flavour in salads.

COWSLIP

PAIGLE, PETERKEYS, PALSYWORT, COWSTRIPLINGS

Height 10–30 cm/4–12 in ✤ April–May

Primula veris
L *primus*, prime, first-blooming
L *veris*, spring-flowering

Delicately perfumed perennial with a rosette of hairy wrinkled toothed leaves, sharply narrowed near stalk like a short-handled spoon. Flowers in clusters usually drooping to one side, each on a leafless stalk. Pale green calyx (cup) supports yellow flower, orange in centre. Seed pods persist a long time. Widely used medicinally as a diuretic and expectorant, and as a remedy for rheumatism and gout, coughs, colds, flu and bronchitis, catarrh, kidney complaints, insomnia and migraine. Leaves and flowers used in salads, as pot herbs, and in puddings and tarts.

FLEABANE, COMMON

FLEA-WORT, JOB'S TEARS

Height up to 90 cm/36 in ✤ July–September

Pulicaria dysenterica
L *pulex*, flea (burned plant's smoke wards off fleas); Gk *dusenteros*, afflicted in the bowels (hence use as remedy for dysentery)

A branched hoary perennial with lance-shaped, slightly toothed leaves, green above, downy below, that clutch the stem. Loose clusters of yellow daisy-like flowers head the stems then develop into crowded groups of 'shuttlecock' seeds. This plant grows in moist places throughout Europe where it is used medicinally more than in the UK. The root was once used against dysentery. The whole plant was dried and burnt to drive away fleas; even unburned, it acted as an insecticide. According to Culpeper: 'the smell is supposed delightful to insects and the juice destructive to them'. The Arabs called it Job's Tears because he used it to heal his ulcers.

FLUELLEN, ROUND-LEAVED

MALE FLUELLEN

Height up to 50 cm/20 in, though often prostrate
❀ July–October

Kickxia spuria
L *kickxia*, after J. J. Kickx (1775–1831),
Belgian botanist; L *spuria*, false or bastard

A creeping hairy annual of the toadflax group
that sprawls its broad, hairy, arrow-shaped
leaves along the ground, bearing in its leaf
axils solitary, stalked, 2-lobed snapdragon
flowers, the lower lip yellow, the upper lip
deep purple, and a curved spur. Also found is
sharp-leaved fluellen (*Kickxia elatine*), very
like the round-leaved version but with arrow-
shaped leaves and slightly smaller flowers with
a spur that is less curved. A plant of cultivated
ground, especially on chalk in S. England.
Possible use in homeopathy for cystitis and
diarrhoea, or to induce perspiration.

GOAT'S-BEARD

JACK-GO-TO-BED-AT-NOON, NAP AT NOON,
JOSEPH'S FLOWER

Height 30–70 cm/12–28 in ❀ May–August

Tragopogon pratensis
Gk *tragopogon*, goat's beard
L *pratensis*, of meadows

A perennial and annual herb with a long
brown tap root and a few erect branches
swathed in long pointed grass-like leaves.
Yellow dandelion-like flowers are borne singly
at the end of stem branches, opening very
early and closing around midday. The fruit
is an attractive 'clock', larger and more open
than dandelion. Seeds are windborne on their
own parachutes. A detoxicant, it stimulates
appetite and digestion. Its high insulin
content makes it useful for diabetics. Used as
a vegetable in Gerard's time and still used in
salads, stews and soups. The ripe root is
treated and eaten like salsify. Stems and young
buds are used like spinach.

IRIS, YELLOW

YELLOW FLAG, MEKKINS, DRAGON FLOWER,
FLEUR DE LYS

Height 40–152 cm/16–60 in ❀ **June–August**

Iris pseudacorus
Iris, in Greek mythology, goddess of the
rainbow; L *pseudacorus*, false acorus (a
different kind of iris)

A stout perennial with an underground
horizontal tuber. Its stiff broad sword-shaped
leaves have a raised midriff and parallel veins.
Strong round stems bear successions of large
yellow flowers with broad oval falls and erect
standards. Large erect seed pods contain many
brown seeds that float for dispersal. Common
in damp lowland places. Poisonous when raw,
so other species are preferred medicinally.
Thought to avert evil – hung over doors in
Ireland on Corpus Christi, and in France on
St John's Eve. Roasted seeds once made into
coffee. Rhizomes yield a black dye and ink.

MARSH-MARIGOLD

GOWAN, KINGCUP, MAYBLOB, WATER BLOBS

Height 30–60 cm/12–24 in ❀ **March–June**

Caltha palustris
L *caltha* from Gk *calathos*, cup
L *palustris*, of marshy or swampy ground

A hairless tufted perennial of marsh and damp
woods. Large glossy heart-shaped leaves rise
on long stalks from the base. Upper leaves on
hollow flower stems are stalkless. Flowers, up
to 2.5 cm/1 inch across or more, have glossy
yellow petals with many yellow stamens but
no green sepals. Fruits are a cluster of pods
with many seeds. This plant grew in England
before the Ice Age. On May Day it was hung
over byre doors to increase the fertility of
cattle and to keep off evil spirits. In medieval
England it was included in a cure for eruptive
rash. In the USA it is eaten as a spring
vegetable. The petals produce a yellow dye.

MELILOT, RIBBED

YELLOW MELILOT, SWEET CLOVER

Height up to 2.5 m/90 in ❀ June–October

Melilotus officinalis
Gk *meli*, honey; Gk *lotos*, name for various
leguminous plants; L *officinalis*, used by
apothecaries for medicinal purposes

A spreading hairless annual or perennial with
upright much-branched stems and trifoliate
leaves with oval toothed leaflets. Yellow pea-
flowers borne in slender erect well-spaced
racemes. Oval pod has single seed. A fodder
crop introduced from W. Europe, now a weed
common on wasteland near cultivation. Also
found is the similar White Melilot (*Melilotus
albus*) formerly cultivated as Bokhara Clover.
Introduced from the Continent, probably by
herbalists. The dried herb used in ointment
for wounds and ulcers, in baths to assuage
melancholy, the juice for eye infections, and
taken to relieve flatulence. A rich source of
wild honey.

MIGNONETTE, WILD

Height 30–60 cm/12–24 in ❀ May–September

Reseda lutea
L *resedare*, to calm or soothe; L *lutea*, yellow

A branched native biennial or perennial
similar to Weld. Narrow lance-shaped leaflets
with wavy edges and a loose spike of yellow
flowers. Seeds are in erect capsules. With its
musky odour, the plant is different from the
sweet-perfumed garden species. Despite Pliny's
reference to its use as part of an ointment to
ease the pain of bruises, other possible
medicinal uses are obscure.

MULLEIN, DARK

BLACK MULLEIN

Height up to 100 cm/40 in ✤ June–September

Verbascum nigrum
L *verbascum*, corruption of L *barbascum*, hairy,
bearded (because plant is woolly)
L *nigrum*, black, dark; OFr *moleine*, soft

A hairy biennial, but not mealy like Great
Mullein. A tall spike with stalked, large, dark-
green leaves, the lower heart-shaped, the
upper smaller. Yellow 5-petalled flowers with
purple hairs on stamens and dark spots at base
of petals. Ovate seeds in a hairy rounded
ovary. Favours chalky banks. Culpeper says
'good for coughs, spitting of blood, and other
affections of the breast; they are likewise
good for griping and colic pains; outwardly
used in fomentations or fumigations, they
are reckoned a specific against the pains
and swelling of the haemorrhoids or piles'.
Poisonous to animals.

NIPPLEWORT

Height 22.5–60 cm/9–24 in ✤ June–October

Lapsana communis
Gk *lapsana*, cress or mustard (suggesting
resemblance to member of mustard family)
L *communis*, common

An annual plant with a many-branched,
upright stem, and large, toothed, terminal
pointed oval leaves with smaller lobes or
wings below. Upper leaves are shorter and
lance-shaped. Tough wiry stems are hollow,
but do not have a milky sap. Numerous yellow
flowers are borne erect in loose-branched
clusters, from nipple-shaped buds. Brown
curved seeds do not have hairs or parachutes.
Differentiate from Wall Lettuce by leaf shapes.
The Nuremberg physician and botanist
Joachim Camerarius in 1588 called this plant
Papillus 'because it is good to heal the ulcers
of the nipples of women's breasts'. John
Parkinson translated this into Nipplewort.
Also used as a salad plant.

PARSNIP, WILD

PARSNIP

Height up to 150 cm/60 in   ❀ June–September

Pastinaca sativa
L *pastinaca*, food dug from the ground
L *sativa*, cultivated

A rough, hairy, tall biennial umbellifer that
emits a pungent aroma when crushed. Rising
from a familiar tap-root, a furrowed angular
stem bears 5–11 bi-pinnate, finely toothed
leaves with broad toothed leaflets. It bears
umbrellas of tiny yellow unsepalled flowers.
Fruits ovate. A European native plant, its
root was described by Gerard as 'small, hard,
woodie and not fit to be eaten'. Roman
Emperor Tiberius had them imported from the
Rhine area. Used to ease stitch and wind. A
strong decoction of the root claimed to be
good for kidney disorders, while the oil of the
seeds administered as a cure for fever. It makes
a palatable wine.

PIMPERNEL, YELLOW

WOOD LOOSESTRIFE, STAR FLOWER (Wiltshire),
MARY'S CLOVER (Eire)

Height 2–10 cm/1–4 in   ❀ May–August

Lysimachia nemorum
After King Lysimachus of Sicily who
recommended this herb for treating wounds
L *nemorum*, of woods; Pimpernel from L
bipinella, double-winged as in leaves of Burnets

An evergreen perennial with slender crawling
stems that bear opposite, pointed-oval, pale
green leaves on very short stalks. Slender
stemmed saucer-shaped 5-petalled yellow star-
like flowers rise singly from the main stems.
Grows in damp deciduous woodland and near
to water. Can be confused with garden escape
Creeping Jenny (*Lysimachia nummularia*)
which has more rounded leaves, and bowl-
shaped flowers. An astringent and good for
open wounds, its use is limited, as *Lysimachia
nummularia* is more effective.

41

PINEAPPLEWEED

SCENTED MAYWEED, RAYLESS MAYWEED,
PINEAPPLE MAYWEED

Height 5–25 cm/2–10 in ❀ May–October

Matricaria discoidea
L *matricaria*, mother care (used for uterine
infections); Gk *diskos* + *-oid*, disc-shaped

A bushy, hairless, strongly apple-scented
annual with fine 2–3-pinnate segmented
threadlike leaves. The unrayed flower heads
consist of closely bunched 4-toothed yellow-
green florets in an acorn-like cup. Seeds
spread rapidly, so plants often found in
colonies; it now flourishes particularly in
farmyards and trampled gateways. A
pernicious weed that blistered hands and feet
during harvest. Seldom used nowadays, but
once used for worms, or as a sedative, and for
the relief of spasms. It was also made into an
ointment for old sores.

PLOUGHMAN'S-SPIKENARD

HORSE HEAL, CINNAMON ROOT

Height 15–120 cm/6–48 in ❀ July–September

Inula conyzae
Inula, L name for *Elecampane* (member of the
fleabane family); Gk *conyza*, dust or powder
(for insecticide); Spikenard, a costly aromatic
ointment from the East; Ploughman's, humble

An erect, hairy, perennial, purplish stem
branched mainly at top. Leaves like foxglove,
finely toothed, upper ones unstalked. Small
numerous flower-heads dull yellow, usually
unrayed with purple inner flower bracts in a
flat cluster. Seeds tiny parachutes. Used as an
infusion for bronchitis, stomach disorders,
gallbladder problems, lack of appetite and
anorexia. Not in common use. Gerard called it
Cinnamon Root because of its aroma. Once
hung up to drive away fleas and gnats.

PRIMROSE

EASTER ROSE, BUTTER ROSE

Height 5–15 cm/2–6 in   ✿ March–June

Primula vulgaris
From L *primus*, prime, first-blooming
L *vulgaris*, common

A perennial with a low rosette of crinkly oval
leaves tapered to the base, soft and downy
below. Pale yellow solitary flowers, slightly
darker in throat. Highly scented. Sticky seeds
carried by ants to germinate where dispersed.
Prefers shady locations such as woods,
coppices, under hedges, usually on heavy
soils. Used in preparing love potions, driving
out worms, and to dye pace eggs. Primrose
tea taken for rheumatism, gout, arthritis and
migraine. Root decoction used against coughs,
catarrhs, bronchitis, headache, jaundice
and ringworm. Used to decorate houses and
barns on May Eve. Posies used to be sold in
markets. Flowers decorated salads and sweets,
crystallised for use in puddings.

RAGWORT, COMMON

RAGWEED, STINKING WILLIE, ST JAMES WORT,
MARE'S FART

Height 30–120 cm/12–48 in   ✿ June–October

Senecio jacobaea
L *senex*, old man; L *jacobaea*, of St James,
patron saint of horses

A hairless biennial with furrowed erect much-
branched stems. Lower leaves stalked and
deeply pinnate, upper leaves clasp stem.
Flower heads of flat clusters of yellow daisy-
like flowers with a ragged look. Seeds have
parachutes of white hairs. Irish and Scots
believed fairies rode the stalks – later witches
took over! Leaves contain an alkaloid poison
that destroys the liver, yet were once used in a
mild infusion to cure 'staggers', an infection of
the brain and spinal cord of domestic animals.
A noxious weed as far as farmers and stock-
keepers are concerned. The national emblem
of the Isle of Man.

ROCK-ROSE, COMMON

SUN FLOWER, SUN ROSE

Height 5–30 cm/2–12 in ❀ May–September

Helianthemum nummularium
Gk *helios*, sun; Gk *anthos*, flower
L *nummularium*, coin-shaped, circular

A prostrate evergreen sub-shrub. Branches
spread from a woody base. Small lance-shaped
leaves, often curled over and with small
stipules at base, green above, greyish and hairy
below. 5-petalled golden-yellow flowers in
groups of up to 12 per stem, often with an
orange blotch at base of petals. On rocky or
grassy limestone and chalk. Unscented flowers
open in sunshine. When dull, closed petals
push pollen-covered stamens on to style for
self-pollination. According to Pliny, the
wise men of Silicia and the Kings of Persia
anointed their bodies with it boiled with lion's
fat, a little saffron and date wine to make
them look handsome.

ST JOHN'S-WORT, PERFORATE

DEVIL'S BANE, COMMON ST JOHN'S-WORT

Height 30–90 cm/12–36 in ❀ July–September

Hypericum perforatum
Gk *hyper*, above; Gk *eikon*, picture (hung
above images to ward off evil spirits)
L *perforatum*, perforated
OE *wort*, plant or root

A hairless perennial with a creeping root.
Its stem has two raised ridges. Opposite
transparent-dotted leaves have elliptical
clear veins. Large clusters of dainty yellow
5-petalled flowers have black dots and streaks
on the petals and edges of the pointed green
sepals. Fruit is a 3-celled capsule. Knights
of St John used it to heal wounds, as the
'perforations' were said to resemble wounds.
A cough cure, helpful for catarrh and bed-
wetting. Stimulates kidneys. Still used against
depression, but over-use may be dangerous if
taken with other medications. NB: several
related species with slight variations.

SILVERWEED

GOOSE TANSY, BREAD AND CHEESE

Height 5–25 cm/2–10 in   ❀ May–August

Potentilla anserina
L *potentilla*, quite powerful (as a medicinal
herb); L *anserina*, relating to geese or meadows

A creeping perennial with a branched stock
producing rooting stolons like strawberries.
Pinnate leaves have 6–12 pairs of toothed
leaflets, alternate large and small and hairy.
Solitary long-stalked flowers have 5 yellow
notched petals twice as long as sepals. Same
medical uses as Creeping Cinquefoil. Plant
steeped in buttermilk removed freckles. Used
in a number of proprietary medicines. Less
astringent than Tormentil and gentler with
diarrhoea. Before potatoes, roots were eaten
boiled, raw or dried and ground into meal for
bread and porridge.

SOW-THISTLE, PERENNIAL

CORN SOW-THISTLE, FIELD MILK-THISTLE

Height up to 150 cm/60 in   ❀ July–September

Sonchus arvensis
Gk *sonchos*, thistle; L *arvensis*, of cultivated
fields

A tall, creeping perennial with a milky juice,
bearing a furrowed erect stem with clasping,
lance-shaped, pinnately lobed, spiny-edged
leaves, greyish beneath. Loose terminal
clusters of yellow dandelion-like flowers
develop into 'shaving brushes' of brown seeds
with white 'parachutes'. Grows in damp,
disturbed or cultivated ground all over Europe.
The leaves can be used as a poultice for open
wounds. The young leaves are eaten raw in
salads after the leaf prickles are removed, or
they can be parboiled in a little water to
remove the bitter taste.

THISTLE, CARLINE
BOAR'S THROAT, EVERLASTINGS

Height 15–30 cm/6–12 in, but can be stemless
❀ July–September

Carlina vulgaris
L *Carolinus* from Carolus, Charles (named
after Charlemagne); L *vulgaris*, common

A stiff prickly biennial with a branched stem
and a rosette only in its first year. Alternate
stem leaves, prickly, thistle-like, lower ones
downy. Flowers, solitary or up to 5, rayless but
with spiny leaf-like outer bracts like rays that
fold over in rain. Fawn-coloured dead flowers
last all winter. When Charlemagne's army was
suffering from plague, an angel told him to fire
an arrow for a cure. It landed on this thistle
with which he treated and healed his army.
Mildly diuretic and antibiotic, it stimulates
perspiration and relieves spasms. Root stock,
collected in autumn, shredded or semi-dried,
still used in proprietary medicines for gallbladder and digestive disorders.

TOADFLAX, COMMON
FLAX WEED, GALLWORT, BUTTER AND EGGS,
BUNNY MOUTHS

Height 23–76 cm/9–30 in ❀ June–October

Linaria vulgaris
Gk *linon*; L *linum*, flax; L *vulgaris*, common
Toad, worthless (cf dog or horse)

A blue-green perennial with erect stems rising
from a creeping rootstock. Alternate lance-
shaped leaves bear basal bracts. Yellow
snapdragon flowers hug a tight spike. Each
flower has a 3-lobed tube with two orange
spots that ends in a long spur, and a 2-lobed
upper petal. Oval capsules containing
flattened winged seeds are larger than the
corolla. A diuretic and purgative that induces
perspiration. Essence used for diarrhoea and
cystitis; also for jaundice, constipation, dropsy,
and haemorrhoids. Culpeper says it was put
into chickens' drinking water 'to cure them
of gall and to relieve them when drooping'.

TORMENTIL

ENGLISH SARSAPARILLA

Height 5–50 cm/2–20 in ❀ **May–September**

Potentilla erecta
L *potentilla*, quite powerful (as a medicinal
herb); L *erecta*, upright; common name is
diminutive of L *tormentum*, torment
(suggesting analgesic use)

A slender, often prostrate, downy perennial
with a stout woody rootstock. Stalked basal
leaves that usually die before the flowers
appear have 3 toothed leaflets, although bracts
make them look like 5 leaflets. Unstalked
upper leaves are similar. Stalked 4-petalled
yellow flowers are carried in loose clusters. Up
to 20 seeds held in a small solid cup. A highly
astringent herb long used for toothache,
diarrhoea, fevers and cholera, and as a
compress for minor burns, grazes and sunburn.
In Guernsey, a remedy for paralysis and quinsy.
With more tannin than oak bark, it was used
for tanning hides. Its roots yield a red dye.

VETCHLING, MEADOW

MEADOW PEA, OLD GRANNY'S SLIPPER-SLOPPERS, YELLOW TARE-TINE

Height 30–120 cm/12–48 in ❀ **June–August**

Lathyrus pratensis
Gk *lathyros*, pea; L *pratensis*, meadow

A sprawling shrubby perennial of grassy
places, hedges, woods and verges. A creeping
root-stock throws up many clump-forming
shoots. Its weak square stems bear tendrils, but
support themselves mainly on nearby grasses.
Lance-shaped leaves are in pairs, each with a
weak tendril, and leaf-like arrow-shaped bracts
at the base. 6–12 pea flowers are borne on
long stalks rising above other vegetation.
Hairless seeds in flattish pods. This member
of the pea family is often sown as a fodder crop
and to enrich the soil, root nodules producing
nitrogen to aid the growth of other plants such
as cereal crops.

YELLOW-RATTLE

HEN PEN, PENNY GRASS, HAY RATTLE,
POTS AND PANS

Height 10–60 cm/4–24 in ❀ **May–August**

Rhinanthus minor
Gk *rhis*, *rhinos*, nose; Gk *anthos*, flower (petal
tube like a hooked nose)

An annual semi-parasite that fixes its roots on
to adjacent grasses from which it takes water
and minerals. A single upright stem, often
branched and spotted black, bears opposite
dark-green, rough and toothed leaves. Yellow
hooded flowers are arranged in opposite pairs
above toothed leaf-like bracts. Open-mouthed
flowers bear 2 violet teeth. When ripe, loose
seeds rattle in pods. Quite common in old
meadows and pastures. Gerard records that it
was unprofitable, presumably as a medicine. In
Lancashire, mothers gave their babies bunches
of the ripe plants as rattles.

YELLOW-WORT

Height 10–60 cm/4–24 in ❀ **June–September**

Blackstonia perfoliata
Blackstonia after eighteenth-century English
botanist and apothecary John Blackstone
L *perfoliata*, the stem appears to have grown
through the middle of a single leaf

A greyish-green annual with a basal rosette of
waxy-grey pointed oval leaves, and an upright
stem. Opposite pointed oval leaves are fused
into one apparently pierced by the stem.
Yellow flowers with 6–8 petal lobes top erect
branches in loose clusters rather like the
Centaury to whose family they belong.
Flowers close in early afternoon. Possibly used,
like Centaury, for fevers, wounds, worms and
skin afflictions. Culpeper specifies its use for
bad temper and nervous disorders.

ANEMONE, WOOD

WINDFLOWER, THUNDER FLOWER,
SMELL FOXES

Height 5–30 cm/2–12 in ❀ March–May

Anemone nemorosa
Anemone from Gk *anemos*, wind. In Gk
mythology, the nymph Anemone was
transformed into a flower by the jealous
goddess Flora; L *nemorosa*, of the woods

Slender stems rise from underground tubers.
Two-thirds of way up, stem has a ring of 3
leaves each with 3 toothed segments. White
flowers tinged pink open only in sunshine.
Seed head is a ball of 10–30 downy fruits.
Musky smell. An ancient woodland indicator.
Leaves used for poultices, for washing ulcers
and sores and for leprosy. Chewing the roots
dispelled lethargy, and ointment made
from the leaves used for clearing ulcers
and inflamed eyes. Used rarely now, except
as an external palliative for arthritis. The
juice, especially of roots, bitter and poisonous.

ANGELICA, WILD

GHOST KEX

Height 60–300 cm/24–120 in ❀ June–September

Angelica sylvestris
Med L *angelica*, angelic herb (for its medicinal
properties); L *sylvestris*, woodland

A tall perennial of damp places with ridged,
hollow, purplish stems. Large divided leaves
with toothed leaflets have an inflated sheath
where they join the stem. Large umbrellas of
pinkish white flowers in globular clusters rise
on separate stems from large sheaths.
Flattened oval fruits have wings to aid
dispersal. The native British herb is not so
effective as the cultivated species, yet it has
been used as a digestive herb for flatulence
and stomach conditions, and for clearing the
eyes, ears and teeth. Chewing the root was
recommended in London during the 1665
plague. Like Sweet Cicely, it sweetens sour
fruit, such as gooseberry and rhubarb, but it
yields too much sugar to be safe for diabetics.

BEDSTRAW, HEDGE

Height 15–38 cm/6–15 in ❀ **June–August**

Galium mollugo
Gk *gala*, milk; *mollugo* from L *mollis*, soft,
pliable

A scrambling hairless perennial with square,
smooth stems. Pale green, pointed, lance-
shaped, single-veined leaves are arranged in
whorls of 6–8 up the stem. Branched loose
clusters of white flowers terminate the stems
and branches. Pairs of smooth globular fruits
turn black when ripe. Grows mainly in
hedgerows and verges. Like Lady's Bedstraw it
was once used for dropsy, renal infections and
stomach disorders. It has been a useful source
of dye, the leaves producing a yellow hue, and
the roots, mixed with wood ash and crowberry
or cranberry fruits, yielding a beautiful scarlet.

BINDWEED, FIELD

BINDWEED, BELLBINE, CORNBINE,
DEVIL'S GUTS

Height 20–60 cm/8–24 in ❀ **June–September**

Convolvulus arvensis
L *convolvere*, to twine
L *arvensis*, of cultivated fields

An invasive perennial weed of cultivation
and waste ground. Extensive often deep white
roots throw up scrambling or twining stems
that strangle other plants for support.
Alternate arrow-shaped leaves on slim stalks.
Pink or white funnel-shaped flowers with
white stripes above and wide mauve stripes
below smell sweetly of almonds. Globular fruit
has 2–4 seeds. A strong purgative, its flowers
give a rich orange or yellow tint to water that
is deepened by the addition of alum and
alkalis.

BRYONY, WHITE

ENGLISH MANDRAKE, WILD NEP

Height up to 400 cm/160 in ☘ May–September

Bryonia dioica
Gk *bryonia*, sprouter, or Gk *bruein*, to swell
or teem (referring to its rate of growth)
Gk *dioica*, two dwellings (male stamens and
female pistils are on separate plants)

A scrambling, climbing perennial with springy
tendrils to support it, often stretching several
yards along hedgerows. The brittle wiry stems
bear alternate, stalked, vine-shaped, 5-lobed
leaves. Open clusters of greenish-white, 5-
petalled flowers (male and female on separate
plants) develop red berries that, like the whole
plant, are very poisonous. A southern plant
of hedges and scrubland. Used as an antidote
to leprosy. Culpeper said it was good for
headiness, cramps and gravel but warned
about its toxicity. No longer in homeopathic
use. Charlatans used to sell the roots as true
mandrake roots with aphrodisiac qualities.

CAMPION, BLADDER

SPATLING POPPIE

Height 25–90 cm/10–36 in ☘ May–August

Silene vulgaris
Gk *silene* from Gk *sialon*, saliva (gummy
exudation on stems) or from Silenus, the
intoxicated foster-father of Bacchus
L *vulgaris*, common

An upright perennial with a greyish look.
All stems bear opposite pointed oval leaves
with hairy margins and a terminal spray of
distinctive white flowers with deeply lobed
petals. The net-veined sepals that form the
inflated calyx are pinched in below the 5
petals to form the bladder. Seeds are globular.
A common plant of drier ground where there
is little competition from tall grasses. The
flowers emit a clove-like perfume in the
evening. Bumble bees unable to enter the
narrow-necked calyx bite holes in the sides to
get at the nectar. The leaves and young shoots
can be used in salads, soups and sauces.

CAMPION, WHITE

Height 30–80 cm/12–32 in   ❀ May–October

Silene latifolia
Gk *silene* from Gk *sialon*, saliva (gummy
exudation on stems) or from Silenus, the
intoxicated foster-father of Bacchus
L *latifolia*, broad-leaved

A sticky annual or short-lived perennial.
Opposite, broad, lance-shaped, hairy, stalked
leaves, the upper ones unstalked. Stems are
topped by small loose clusters of white, deeply
notched, 5-petalled night-scented flowers up
to 2 cm/1 in across, very attractive to insects.
Seeds in a slightly inflated calyx. Hybridises
with Red Campion. Thrives on uncultivated
land in Europe and S. Britain. Medicinal
properties limited, but Culpeper suggests many
applications for internal bleeding, urinary
problems, cleaning wounds, and stings of
'venomous beasts'.

CANDYTUFT, WILD

Height 5–24 cm/2–9 in   ❀ May–August

Iberis amara
Gk *Iberis*, from Iberia; L *amara*, bitter

A rare southern plant but not uncommon in
the chalky Chilterns. An upright, slightly
hairy annual with narrow, pinnately lobed
leaves issuing alternately up a purplish stem.
Large flat heads of mauvy-white flowers crown
dark stalks, the petals of unequal size. In
homeopathy, a tincture is made from the ripe
seeds for gout, rheumatism, and to allay heart
conditions. Useful for bronchitis, asthma and
dropsy. Overdoses induce giddiness, diarrhoea
and nausea.

CARROT, WILD

BIRD'S NEST

Height 60–120 cm/24–48 in ❀ June–September

Daucus carota
Daucus, from Gk *dais*, to burn (pungent
and stimulating qualities)
Celt *carota*, red of colour

From a small, hard, whitish tap root quite
unlike its garden cultivar, erect branched
hoary stems bear finely divided leaves. The
flowers in small terminal rosettes radiate on
their own stems from the top of the main stem
to form a multiple head of white rosettes, the
centre one often purple. Short spiny fruits. A
plant of downland and roadsides. An infusion
of the whole herb has been used to treat
dropsy, kidney and bladder infections. Carrot
tea believed to help gout. Seeds are useful for
flatulence, coughs and hiccoughs. Culpeper
stated that the flower, boiled in wine and
drunk, 'helpeth conception'. Can be made
into jam and wine.

CATMINT, WILD

CATNEP

Height 30–90 cm/12–36 in ❀ June–September

Nepeta cataria
L *nepeta*, from Nepi, an ancient Tuscan town
where it was said to be prolific; L *cataria*, of
cats; Gk *kalaminthe*, beautiful mint

A perennial root bears tall, mealy, square
stems with opposite toothed, heart-shaped,
hoary leaves that smell strongly of mint. The
white or pink-spotted short-stalked orchid-like
flowers grow in whorls. Though often seen
as a garden escape, the truly wild plant is
becoming much less frequent. Used in France,
formerly in UK, as tea. The flowering tops
are infused to lower fevers, as a light sedative,
to alleviate nervous headaches and coughs.
Culpeper recommended the juice for bruises,
the leaves for piles, and a decoction of the
whole plant for head-scurf and scabs. Loved
by cats, hated by rats! Young shoots used for
salads in France.

DEAD-NETTLE, WHITE

WHITE ARCHANGEL, ADAM AND EVE
IN THE BOWER

Height 20–60 cm/8–24 in ☞ March–November

Lamium album
Gk *laimos*, throat (referring to the shape of the
flowers); L *album*, white

A hairy faintly aromatic creeping perennial,
usually in wide colonies. Square, hollow, hairy
stems bear opposite pairs of toothed, heart-
shaped leaves like Stinging Nettle on short
stalks. Whorls of white flowers rise from leaf
nodes, upper lip hairy, lower has a large
notched middle lobe and 2 smaller lateral
lobes. Turn the flower upside down and under
the white upper lip of the corolla the black
and gold stamens, side by side, are Adam and
Eve. Fruits are 4 nutlets in the sepal-tube.
Once used against diarrhoea, varicose veins,
haemorrhoids, the King's Evil (scrofula) and
to reduce menstrual bleeding.

DROPWORT

Height 15–45 cm/6–18 in ☞ May–August

Filipendula vulgaris
L *filum*, thread; L *pendula*, hanging (refers to
threads connecting root tubers); L *vulgaris*,
common

Tubers develop on a thread-like root away
from parent. Erect stem with dark green
toothed pinnate leaves, mainly as a basal
rosette. Light cream flowers with 6 petals,
purplish below, unscented. Buds globular, like
dewdrops. Downy nutlet fruits ribbed but not
twisted. This is the downland form of
Meadowsweet with fewer, unscented flowers.

ENCHANTER'S-NIGHTSHADE

CINDERELLEN, PHILTREWORT,
WITCHES' POISON

Height 15–70 cm/6–27 in ❀ June–August

Circaea lutetiana
After Circe, the beautiful sorceress who
turned Ulysses' crew into pigs; L *Lutetia*, Paris

A slightly downy perennial with long slim
stolons. Erect hairy stems have opposite,
toothed, pointed oval leaves with a channel
along top edge. Leafless spikes of sparse flowers
with 2 petals deeply notched and 2 lobed
stigma. Hairy fruits have hooks for clinging to
animals. Always associated with magic, the
Anglo-Saxons called it Aelfthone, a
protection against elves. Belongs to the
Willowherb family, not related to the true
Nightshades. Being rich in tannin, it may
have been used as an astringent.

EYEBRIGHT

OCULARIS, OPHTHALMICA

Height up to 30 cm/12 in ❀ June–September

Euphrasia spp.
Named after Euphrosyne, in Greek mythology
the Grace of gladness and mirth

A hairy annual with erect stems rising from a
creeping branch. Toothed oval leaves dark
green and hairy. 2-lipped flowers in leafy
spikes. Lower lip has 3 narrow lobes, and
purple lines leading to a yellow patch. Lilac
upper lip also lined. In seventeenth century
William Coles claimed the resemblance to
bloodshot eye indicated a cure for eye diseases.
Culpeper said eye drops made from the plant
(still widely sold by herbalists) improved
eyesight and memory. The herb is bitter and
astringent, and is made into poultices for
coughs, colds, sore throats and catarrh. An
ingredient in mixed herbal tobaccos for
asthma.

FEVERFEW

Height 25–60 cm/10–24 in ❀ June–September

Tanacetum parthenium
Tanacetum is its medieval L name, derived
from Gk *athanatos*, immortal; Gk *parthenos*,
virgin (traditional use in relieving menstrual
cramps); common name from L *febrifuga*,
fever-dispelling

A downy perennial with erect stems bearing
pinnately divided yellowish-green toothed,
aromatic leaves. Upper part of stem branched.
Branches bear loose flat-topped clusters of
daisy-like flowers, yellow with white rays.
Ribbed brown seeds have papery edges.
Once in common use, now used as an
insect repellent and for migraine. Gerard
recommended it for melancholy, phlegm,
dizziness and vertigo, also 'for such as be sad,
pensive, and without speech'. Culpeper
records: 'Venus has commended it to her
sisters to be a general strengthener of wombs'.

FLAX, FAIRY

PURGING FLAX, LADY'S LINT

Height 5–20 cm/2–8 in ❀ May–September

Linum catharticum
L *linum*, flax, linen; L *catharticum*, purging

An erect slender annual with wiry stems rising
from threadlike roots bearing opposite leaves,
each with a single vein. White, 5-petalled
flowers are borne in a loose branched head.
Fruits, almost spherical, have tiny brown
seeds. A purgative, emetic, diuretic and worm
cure. A tincture of the whole plant is used
against bronchitis, piles and amenorrhoea, and
was once taken as an infusion against liver
disorders, constipation and rheumatic pains.
Not now used because too violent. Grows on
short turf.

HEMLOCK

POISON PARSLEY, SPOTTED HEMLOCK,
BAD MAN'S OATMEAL, POISON SNAKEWEED

Height 90–210 cm/48–84 in   ✿ June–August

Conium maculatum
Gk *coneion*, hemlock; L *maculatum*, blotched,
spotted

A tall elegant umbellifer with a smooth stem
with purple blotches, and numerous finely
divided 2-pinnate dull green leaves. When
crushed they give off an unpleasant smell. The
seeds are globular with wavy ridges. Poisonous
– can produce paralysis, loss of speech,
asphyxia and even death, yet it is recognised
as an effective drug to treat neuralgia and
rheumatic complaints. Once used to treat
cholera, hernia, pleurisy, epilepsy and double
vision. The plant was used for judicial
executions in ancient Greece, most famously
that of Socrates.

HOGWEED

KECK, COW PARSNIP

Height up to 300 cm/115 in   ✿ May–September

Heracleum sphondylium
After Heracles (Hercules) who used it
medicinally; L *sphondylium*, rounded

A stout hairy perennial with tall hollow ridged
stems. Large hairy pinnate leaves have
coarsely toothed leaflets – terminal and
opposite pairs – with stalks sheathing stems.
Large flattened umbrellas of up to 20 branched
bunches of white flowers with irregular outer
florets. Seeds are oval to round, flattened, with
a slight wing on sides. Culpeper says the seeds
are useful for coughs, shortness of breath,
falling sickness, jaundice, phlegm and liver
problems. Seeds and roots boiled in oil and
rubbed on the head help frenzy, lethargy and
shingles. Flower juice cleans runny ears.
Extracts still used in proprietary medicines for
laryngitis and bronchitis. Once fed to pigs –
some think it smells like pigs!

MAYWEED, SCENTLESS

CORN FEVERFEW, SCENTLESS CHAMOMILE

Height 15–45 cm/6–18 in ❁ April–October

Tripleurospermum inodorum
L *tripleurospermum*, three-ribbed seed
L *inodorum*, scentless, without odour

A sprawling, branching annual of waste ground with deeply divided slender leaves. Single flat daisy-like flowers are borne on long flower stems, the central florets yellow, disc florets white. Ribbed seeds. Called Mayweed because it was helpful to maidens – nothing to do with the month of May. As name suggests, used for all kinds of female complaints. In Finland an infusion is used for consumption.

MEADOWSWEET

BRIDEWORT, QUEEN OF THE MEADOW

Height 60–120 cm/24–48 in ❁ June–September

Filipendula ulmaria
L *filum*, thread (roots); L *pendula*, hanging
L *ulmus*, elm (which the leaves were said to resemble)

Clusters of stems rise from tubers. Dark green leaves, whitish below, are crumpled and wrinkled like Elm leaves. Each leaf has up to 5 pairs of leaflets. Purplish, rising to pale green, stems bear frothy upright clusters of 5-petalled flowers with an almond scent. Fruits fused together into a spiral (old name was *Spiraea*). Common in woods and damp places. A strewing herb, especially for weddings, also used in brides' garlands and posies. Contains salicylic acid (aspirin). Used against diarrhoea, toothache, rheumatism and influenza. The root was once used for flour, and dried flowers make 'tobacco'.

MUSTARD, GARLIC

JACK-BY-THE-HEDGE, HEDGE GARLIC

Height 30–60 cm/12–24 in ❀ April–June

Alliaria petiolata
L *allium*, garlic; L *petiolata*, stalked

An erect unbranched perennial plant with stalked heart-shaped leaves near base, triangular above. When crushed they emit a garlic odour. Erect stem bears a cluster of small white flowers whose pungent garlic smell attracts midges and hoverflies. Erect fruits in long green seed pods. In June this plant attracts the green caterpillars of the Orange Tip butterfly. A diuretic, it also kills worms. Infusion helps bronchitis, eczema, skin disorders. Herbal compress for cuts and skin ailments. Leaves in salads give garlic flavour without breath smell, and a mustardy aftertaste. Makes a good sauce for fish dishes.

ORCHID, GREATER BUTTERFLY

FOXSTONES

Height 20–60 cm/8–24 in ❀ June–July

Platanthera chlorantha
Gk *platanthera*, flat flower (hence wide or flat anthered); L *chlorantha*, green-flowered

Twin tubers, each forked. A new tuber formed annually as old one dies away. One pair of shiny basal leaves and pairs of narrower unstalked pointed leaves alternate up stem. Vanilla-scented flowers. White narrow oval petals, lower one a strap-like lip, and a 2.5-cm/1-inch down-curved spur. Loose spike of 10–15 flowers. Persists a long time, especially in shade where flowers are greener. Insect-pollinated. Gerard classified it under Foxstones, and considered it of no great use in physic.

PANSY, FIELD

Height up to 40 cm/15 in   ✤ April–October

Viola arvensis
L *viola*, plant name; L *arvensis*, of cultivated
fields

An upright hairy annual of arable land and
waste places, now thriving in set-aside fields.
Our commonest wild pansy. Upright stem
bears oblong bluntly toothed pinnate leaves,
the end lobe largest. Flowers extremely
variable in both size and colour, basically
cream, varied with patches of orange and
streaks of violet. Medical uses obscure, but
has been used as ointment for skin diseases
and internally for bronchitis.

PARSLEY, COW

QUEEN ANNE'S LACE

Height 60–120 cm/24–48 in   ✤ April–June

Anthriscus sylvestris
L *anthriscus*, plant name; L *sylvestris*, woodland

A sturdy perennial with upright furrowed
stems, downy below, hairy above. Fresh,
finely cut leaves have toothed segments,
not aromatic, and unspotted. Upper stem
branched, with smooth-stalked globular
flower-heads forming a flattish umbrella. Fruits
are smooth and long, broad at the base, with
a short beak at the tip. It could be mistaken
for Hemlock and Fool's Parsley – both are
poisonous. The commonest white umbellifer
of road verges and hedge bottoms in late
spring. Few uses – leaves fed to rabbits, stems
used for pea-shooters. Superstition links it
with the Devil.

PARSLEY, FOOL'S

LESSER HEMLOCK, DOG POISON (Somerset),
DEVIL'S WAND (Dorset)

Height 45–100 cm/18–48 in ❀ **June–October**

Aethusa cynapium
Gk *aithos*, fire (fiery, acrid taste); L *aethusa*,
burning one; Gk *kyon*, dog (inferior, hence
fool's)

A hairless biennial resembling both Parsley
and Hemlock. Green finely ridged hollow
stems bear 2-pinnate diamond-shaped leaves.
Umbels of tiny white flowers have drooping
green bracteoles that continue when in broad-
ovoid seed. A weed of cultivated ground. This
is a very poisonous plant (not quite so toxic as
Hemlock) but its use has been recorded as a
sedative, and for diarrhoea and cholera in
children.

PARSLEY, HEDGE

UPRIGHT HEDGE PARSLEY, LACE FLOWER,
DEVIL'S NIGHTCAP, SCABBY HEAD

Height 5–90 cm/2–36 in ❀ **July–September**

Torilis japonica
Gk *torilis*, engraved (fruits); L *japonica*,
Japanese (Asiatic)

A tall, hairy annual, the latest to flower of the
three common white hedgerow umbellifers.
Its stiff upright stems are solid and ridged and
bear coarsely toothed 1–3-pinnate (fern-like,
reminiscent of Cow Parsley) alternate leaves.
Pinkish-white flowers are borne on straight,
spreading, slender stalks in small loose balls
that make up a delicate larger globular cluster.
The egg-shaped fruits are covered with curved,
hooked spines. A common plant of dry
hedgerows, scrubland, woodland edges and
grassy pastures.

PIGNUT

EARTHNUT, STINKY LIPS

Height 22–45 cm/9–18 in ❀ May–August

Conopodium majus
Gk *conos*, cone (root shape); Gk *podium*, foot

Round brown tuber bears erect, slightly ridged
stem with carrot-like leaves that die back
before flowering stem emerges with fine leaves
rising from a strong sheath. Loose clusters
of notched white flowers. Beaked oval fruits.
Common in dry pastures. 'Nuts' grow about
20 cm/8 in below ground. Root tuber can be
eaten, either raw, or cooked to give a parsnip-
like flavour. Much loved and rooted out
by pigs which were once trained like
truffle-hunters to locate them for human
consumption. Shakespeare's Caliban offered
to dig up pignuts with his long nails for his
master Prospero in *The Tempest*.

RAMSONS

WILD GARLIC, RAMPS, BEAR'S GARLIC

Height 8–45 cm/3–18 in ❀ April–June

Allium ursinum
L *allium*, garlic; L *ursinum*, of bears, ursine (fit
only for bears to eat)

An odorous bulbous woodland perennial. 2 or
3 bright green ovate leaves with parallel veins
appear first, then an erect round three-sided
stem bearing a loose ball of white starry
flowers with pointed petals and prominent
stamens. Fruit is globe-shaped in a 3-lobed
ovary. Seeds are black. Fresh leaves may be
eaten raw in salads for high blood pressure.
Used as a flavouring in soups and with
vegetables. Has similar properties to clove
garlic but leaves a bitter aftertaste. The name
Ramsbottom means Ramson Valley, and
Ramsey means Ramson Island.

SANICLE

Height 20–60 cm/8–24 in ❀ May–September

Sanicula europaea
From L *sanus*, healthy, or a corruption of
St Nicholas, a great healer

Hairless perennial with long-stemmed shiny,
deeply cut 5-lobed toothed leaves. Short
staked clusters of pinkish-white flowers.
Roundish fruits covered in clinging hooked
bristles. A vulnerary, it was applied to wounds
and bleeding both internal and external, and
used for skin diseases, mouthwashes, chest
complaints, coughs, catarrh and piles. A
fifteenth-century apothecaries' cure-all drink
of Sanicle, Yarrow and Bugle: 'Bugle holdeth
it open, Mylfoyle clensith, Sanicle helith'.
Called Herbe de St Laurent in France, it is
invoked for burns and scalds, because St
Lawrence was put to death on a grid-iron.

SNEEZEWORT

BACHELORS' BUTTONS

Height 30–60 cm/12–24 in ❀ July–September

Achillea ptarmica
After Achilles, who used it medicinally
Gk *ptarmikos*, causing sneezes (used for snuff)

A hairy perennial with a woody creeping
rootstock. Hairy, angular, erect stems bear
unstalked, sharply lance-shaped leaves with
fine teeth on the margins. Small white-rayed
daisy-like flowers are borne in loose, branched
clusters, the unrayed central florets greenish-
white. Seeds blackish. It grows in damp, grassy
places on acid or neutral soils. Discovered in
Kentish Town, London, by John Gerard who
said its smell was enough to make one sneeze.
Its hot, biting leaves were used to spice up
salads. The roots held in the mouth taste
sharp, cause saliva to flow, and ease toothache.

SNOWFLAKE, SUMMER

LODDON LILY, SNOWFLAKES

Height 60–90 cm/24–36 in ❀ **April–May**

Leucojum aestivum
L *leucojum*, white violet (Hippocrates' name
for a snowflake); L *aestivum*, of summer

A sturdy, clump-forming perennial of the
south of England. Its bright green 2-winged
strap-shaped leaves rise before stalks bearing
lax clusters of 2–6 hanging white bell-flowers
like fat Snowdrops with green markings at the
tips of each equal-sized petal. Anthers orange.
Seeds resemble tiny carrots. As one of its
vernacular names indicates, it grows in and
around Berkshire's River Loddon, its attractive
nature leading to its introduction to other
places, mainly in S. England.

SQUINANCYWORT

QUINSYWORT

Height 5–10 cm/2–4 in ❀ **June–September**

Asperula cynanchica
L *asper*, rough (hairy stems); L *asperula*, little
rough one; Gk *kunanchi* and L *cynanchica*, of
quinsy (lit. 'dog-throttler', referring to the
plant's toxic qualities)

A prostrate hairless slender perennial. Four
ridges on stems make them look square.
Narrow lance-shaped leaves in whorls of 4,
2 of them smaller than the others, up stem.
Flowers in terminal clusters, pink inside,
whitish outside, with long tubed base. Vanilla-
scented. Tiny fruits warted. It favours dry
pastures on limestone or chalk. Found first in
1570 by Flemish botanist De l'Obel at Silbury,
between London and Bath. As indicated
by name, used for curing the quinsy, an
inflammation of the throat and suppuration of
the tonsils. Also used as an astringent gargle.

STAR-OF-BETHLEHEM

DOVE'S DUNG, BETTY-GO-TO-BED-AT-NOON

Height 15–30 cm/6–12 in ❀ May–June

Ornithogalum angustifolium
L *ornithogalum*, bird-milk; L *angustifolium*,
narrow-leaved

A perennial bulb with 6–9 hairless droopy
leaves with a central groove highlighted with
a white stripe. A cluster of white 6-petalled
star-like flowers with a broad green band on
the back crown a round upright stem. Fruits
have 6 ribs. New bulblets form round base.
Truly wild flowers rare, many are garden
escapes. The edible bulbs were collected by
Arabs to feed them on their travels, especially
on their pilgrimages to Mecca. Gerard,
quoting Dioscorides, notes: 'the roots are
eaten both raw and boiled'. Similar species
are Loddon Lily and Bath Asparagus. A
symbol of purity. It grows in profusion in
Palestine, hence its English name.

STITCHWORT, GREATER

HEADACHE, MAY FLOWER, STAR GRASS,
PIXIES, PISKEYS, THUNDER FLOWER

Height 15–60 cm/6–24 in ❀ March–June

Stellaria holostea
L *stellaria*, star; Gk *holosteon*, whole bones

A weak straggly perennial often in groups
in hedgerows and woods. Long square hairy
stems bear narrow stalkless leaves, greyish and
rough-edged. Deeply cleft 5-petalled flowers
are borne in loose clusters on individual stalks.
Sepals are shorter than the petals. Lesser
Stitchwort (*Stellaria graminea*) is a smaller
version, flowering later in the summer. As
name suggests, once used in healing bone
fractures. Gerard said 'drink it in wine with
the powder of acorns against the pain in the
side, stitches and such-like'. Superstition
bestowed it with catastrophic properties –
picking it was supposed to provoke
thunderstorms and to invite snakebites
or even bewitchment.

STRAWBERRY, WILD

ALPINE STRAWBERRY

Height 10–20 cm/4–8 in 🌼 **April–July**

Fragaria vesca
L *fraga*, scent (of fruit); L *vesca*, little

A hairy perennial with rooting runners
throwing up clumps of toothed trefoil leaves,
bright green above, paler below. Flowers on
erect stalks have sepals and petals in whorls
of 5. No gaps between petals. Fruit fleshy.
Diuretic, astringent, laxative in small doses.
Infusion of leaves against arthritis, gall stones,
liver and gum disease, stomach upsets. A tea
substitute when spiced with lemon, cinnamon
or vanilla and sweetened with honey. (The
poisonous leaves of the cultivated strawberry
must not be used.) Blackberry and Strawberry
leaves are fed medicinally to off-colour or
constipated rabbits and guinea pigs. The fruit
is delectable.

TRAVELLER'S-JOY

OLD MAN'S BEARD, BACCY PLANT, WOODBINE, WILD CLEMATIS

Stems up to 30 m/100 ft 🌼 **July–September**

Clematis vitalba
Gk *clematis*, climbing plant
L *vitalba*, white vine

A deciduous woody climber with opposite
toothed 3–5-leaflet leaves on flexible stalks
which twist around adjacent plants for
support. Fragrant greenish-white flowers have
prominent yellow stamens borne in loose
trusses along and at ends of stems. Seeds with
long silvery plumes cluster at stalk heads to
form 'beards'. They persist well into winter.
Grows at woodland edges and in hedgerows
mainly on calcareous ground. Bruised roots
and stems boiled in water and steeped in
sweet oil used as a cure for itch. The stems
were once used by boys as a form of tobacco.
Medieval beggars used the caustic sap to raise
mock wounds, to help them gain alms.

WATER-CRESS

Height 10–38 cm/4–15 in   ❀ May–October

Rorippa nasturtium-aquaticum
Rorippa, from an old Saxon name
L *nasus*, nose; L *tortus*, twisted (Pliny's '*quod
nasum torqueat*' refers to mustard-oil smell of
leaves); L *aquaticum*, living in water

A hairless, creeping, aquatic, winter-green
perennial with often-rooting hollow root
stems. Surface stems bear stalked leaves made
up of 5–11 pointed oval leaflets. 4-petalled
white flowers borne on loose spikes. Netted
seeds in 2 rows in cylindrical pods. Rich in
vitamin C – eaten raw or boiled against scurvy.
Also has many minerals, especially iodine, iron
and phosphorus. A blood cleanser, spring
tonic, diuretic, detoxifier, improving appetite
and relieving indigestion. Used in some
proprietary medicines. Culpeper said that
bruised leaves free face from spots and
blemishes.

WATER-CROWFOOT, CHALKSTREAM

Prostrate/underwater   ❀ June–August

Ranunculus penicillatus
L *ranunculus*, little frog (referring to
preference for damp locations); L *penicillatus*,
brush-like

Hairless, aquatic annual or perennial, similar
to River Water-crowfoot (*Ranunculus fluitans*)
but prefers fast-flowing streams, especially
with limy water. Leaves usually submerged,
with long trailing tresses, although sometimes
5-lobed floating leaves. White buttercup
flower with central yellow 'claws', 20–30 mm,
longer fruit stalks. Stems and leaves may vary
depending on depth and speed of flow of
water.

WATER-DROPWORT, HEMLOCK

Height 60–120 cm/24–48 in ❀ May–August

Oenanthe crocata
Gk *oenanthe*, wine flower (i.e. plant smelling like the vine); L *crocata*, saffron-yellow (dye)

A sturdy, hairless, POISONOUS perennial with large tubers attached by thin root stems or 'drops'. Hollow upright stems are grooved and stout. Glossy triangular leaves with oval lobed and toothed leaflets, the leaf stalks forming a sheath round the stem. Large roundish umbrellas of clustered small white flowers stand erect above the stem. Up to 40 cylindrical seeds on separate short branches. Plant smells of Parsley. Grows near ditches and streams, particularly where there is a little lime in the soil. Locally profuse. Culpeper said the root was good for gravel, urine stoppage, and as a diuretic. Small doses obtained from roots were once used as a cure for gallstones. Used to kill rats and moles. Many records of human and animal fatalities after eating roots.

WOODRUFF

STARGRASS, WOODROWELL, WOODROVE, SWEET WOODRUFF

Height 10–45 cm/4–18 in ❀ April–June

Galium odoratum
Gk *gala*, milk; L *odoratum*, scented

Perennial with a slender creeping rhizome. Erect 4-sided stems unbranched. Leaves with prickly margins arranged in whorls of 6–9 up stem. Pure white flowers in loose heads. Fruits are hooked with tiny bristles. Our only woodland bedstraw, mainly on lime. A long-used herb. Leaves likened to the rowel of a spur (Fr *rovelle*), hence name Woodrove. Medicinal uses against jaundice, liver ailments, migraine, bladder complaints, nerves, insomnia and thromboses. Its scent, like new-mown hay, increases with time. Hung in bunches to freshen air, put in drawers and cupboards to deter moths; used to stuff pillows. Adds flavour to drinks – in Germany, combined with strawberries and hock.

WOOD-SORREL

SPRING BEAUTY, ALLELUJA,
BREAD AND CHEESE

Height 5–15 cm/2–6 in ❋ March–May

Oxalis acetosella
Gk *oxys*, acid or sour; L *acetosella*, slightly acid
Sorrel, sour

A perennial with a creeping rhizome.
Shamrock leaves pale green, purplish below.
Solitary cup-shaped white flowers veined
purple, 5 petals. Slender dark stems. Fruit
a globular capsule. As a medicine it was
prescribed for fevers, scurvy and to aid
menstruation. Bruised leaves applied to cuts
and bruises. Because of its high oxalic acid
content this plant must be used sparingly.
Used for centuries to add flavour to salads
and sauces. The name Alleluja comes from
its appearance at Easter when the Alleluja
is sung, and because its 3-in-1 leaves signify
the Trinity.

YARROW

MILFOIL, SOLDIERS' WOUNDWORT,
NOSE-BLEED

Height up to 60 cm/up to 24 in ❋ June–October

Achillea millefolium
Achilles who used it to stem his soldiers'
bleeding wounds; L *millefolium*, thousand
leaflets; AS *gearwe*, yarrow

An erect hairy perennial with a rough angular
stem branching at the top and bearing long
alternate bi-pinnate (feathery) leaves. White
flowers, often with a lilac tint, like small
daisies are held in loose terminal heads. Tiny
seeds are winged. Has had many uses, against
colds and fevers, purifying the blood, bleeding
piles, kidney disorders and arresting hair loss.
Some Scots shepherds thought it good against
sheep scab. Swedes used it to flavour beer.

BASIL, WILD

Height 22–45 cm/9–18 in ❀ July–September

Clinopodium vulgare
Gk *klinein*, to slope, lean; Gk *podion*, dim.
of Gk *pous*, foot; L *vulgare*, common
L *basilicum* from Gk *basilikon*, royal (hence,
king of herbs)

A hairy aromatic perennial. Erect stems
usually unbranched; oval opposite hairy
leaves, slightly toothed. Faintly scented.
Flowers borne in whorls above leaves with
bristles like bracts that make it look woolly.
Seeds 4 nutlets in a short sepal tube. Grows
on dry grassy banks and in hedgerows on limy
soils. Infusion used for stomach trouble and
enteritis. Indian Brahmins eat a few leaves
after meals to aid digestion. Has been used
to preserve cooked meats and in Egypt it was
scattered over graves. Always popular with
Greek, Italian and French cooks. Hot clove-
like flavour. Used in salads and cooking.

BETONY

BISHOP'S WORT, WOOD BETONY

Height 15–60 cm/6–24 in ❀ June–October

Stachys officinalis
Gk *stakhus*, ear of wheat, spike; L *officinalis*,
used by apothecaries for medicinal purposes
Fr *bétoine* from L *Vettonica*, of the Vettones,
an ancient Iberian tribe

Perennial herb with a short woody root. Erect
hairy stems rise from a persistent basal rosette
of stalked toothed ovate leaves. Upper leaves
unstalked below a dense cylindrical whorl,
often two, of reddish-purple labiate (tubular
2-lipped) flowers. Fruits 4 smooth brown
tricorn nutlets. An ancient herbal remedy.
Treatise written on it by Emperor Augustus's
chief physician, Musa, who claimed it would
cure 47 diseases. Infusions for diarrhoea,
flatulence, phlebitis, arthritis, open wounds,
headaches and tension, coughs and colds.
Dried leaves used as tea, mixed with tobacco
and smoked, and as an ingredient for snuff.

BITTERSWEET

WOODY NIGHTSHADE, FELONWOOD
(against 'felons', whitlows)

Stems creep 20–300 cm/12–115 in
❀ **June–September**

Solanum dulcamara
From L *solamen*, solace, comfort; L *dulcis*,
sweet; L *amarus*, bitter

A scrambling hairy perennial with woody
stems. Leaves are stalked, oval-pointed with
2 narrow lobes at the base. Flowers in loose,
drooping clusters, have 5 swept-back purple
petals with yellow anthers in a cone shape.
Green egg-shaped berries turn from green to
yellow to red as they ripen. Many seeds in
each berry. Plant contains narcotic alkaloid
solanine that tastes bitter then sweet.
Essence relieves spasms and epilepsy. Used in
proprietary medicines against skin diseases,
rheumatic and blood disorders. Overdose can
lead to paralysis of the tongue and finally loss
of speech. Berries can cause sickness if eaten.

COMFREY, COMMON

KNITBONE, BONESET

Height 25–120 cm/10–48 in   ❀ **May–September**

Symphytum officinale
Gk *symphysis*, growing together; Gk *phyton*,
plant; L *officinale*, used by apothecaries for
medicinal purposes
Comfrey from L *confervere*, to boil together

An upright hairy perennial herb. Its tall
branched stem is winged and bears large hairy
broad lance-shaped leaves right up the stem.
Small coiled clusters of nodding bell-shaped
flowers in white, cream, purple or pink droop
from stem-sides and heads. Fruits are glossy
black nutlets. Much used in proprietary
medicines against phlebitis, eczema, mastitis,
haematoma, ulcers and gastritis. The leaves
make good poultices or fomentations against
sprains and bruises, cuts, boils and gangrenous
ulcers. Young shoots are used in salads, soups,
stews, or like asparagus. Roots with Dandelion
and Chicory make a tolerable coffee.

DEAD-NETTLE, RED

DEVIL'S POSIES, PURPLE ARCHANGEL

Height 10–45 cm/4–18 in   ❀ **March–November**

Lamium purpureum
Gk *laimos*, throat (referring to the shape of the
flowers); L *purpureum*, dull red-purple

A sprawling, downy annual with a pungent
smell if crushed. Squarish, often purplish stems
bear wrinkled, bluntly toothed, heart-shaped
leaves with pointed tips in opposite pairs on
short stalks. Pinkish-purple 2-lipped flowers,
the upper lip a hood, the lower 2-lobed, are
borne in leafy clusters up the stem. Pointed
sepals form a cup for 4 nutlet seeds. Bruised
leaves applied to wounds. Herb tea from leaves
eases kidney problems and purifies blood. Has
been used against King's Evil (scrofula) and
the roots boiled in sweet milk to purge
measles. If boiled, can be used as a pot herb
or in pig swill.

GENTIAN, AUTUMN

FELWORT

Height 5–24 cm/2–9 in   ❀ **August–September**

Gentianella amarella
L *gentianella*, little gentian (after Gentius,
King of Illyria, said to have discovered its
medicinal uses for his malaria-stricken troops)
L *amara*, bitter

An upright perennial with simple or branched
stem. Oval leaves in rosette, stem leaves
opposite and pointed. Dull purple trumpet-
shaped flowers in spikes. Petal tube twice as
long as sepal tube, stays on after flowering.
Fruits cylindrical. Used in cures for cramps,
King's Evil (scrofula), bites of mad dogs and
venomous beasts, and loss of appetite.
Apothecaries found this plant just as effective
as the Yellow Gentian, which had been
imported in large amounts from European
alpine countries.

GENTIAN, CHILTERN

Height up to 50 cm/20 in 🌣 August–September

Gentianella germanica
L *gentianella*, little gentian (after Gentius,
King of Illyria, said to have discovered its
medicinal uses for his malaria-stricken troops)
L *germanica*, from Germany

A localised biennial that stretches from its
main UK location in the Chilterns to the
North Hampshire Downs on chalk turf.
Similar to the Autumn Gentian (G. *amarella*)
with which it hybridises freely. Flowers larger
and a rather brighter purple than Autumn
Gentian, with larger and broader petals, the
sepal-tube being broader at the tip, giving
an almost bell-shaped appearance. In the
Chilterns, the pure Autumn Gentian is more
distinctive than the pure Chiltern Gentian
with most hybrids looking like the latter.
This gentian, localised and rare in UK, is
more common in the Alps.

GOAT'S-RUE

HERBA RUTA CAPRARIA, CHEESE-RENNET,
ITALIAN FITCH, FRENCH LILAC

Height up to 90 cm/36 in 🌣 June–September

Galega officinalis
Gk *gala*, milk and Gk *aghein*, to get (hence,
milk-promoter); L *officinalis*, used by
apothecaries for medicinal purposes

A hairless bushy perennial. Upright stems bear
alternate pinnate leaves with 5–8 pairs of
opposite pointed oval leaves. White or lilac
pea-flowers on side stalks. Fruits in cylindrical
pods. Increasingly naturalised on waste and
damp ground. Introduced in sixteenth century
from Italy as a vegetable and a medicinal herb.
Formerly used against plague. Used in fevers,
smallpox and measles, effective against worms,
bites and gout, and a refreshing bath additive.
In northern counties it was once used instead
of rennet in the making of cheese. Widely
cultivated as cattle feed.

GROUND-IVY

ALEHOOF, GILL

Height 10–60 cm/4–24 in ❀ **March–June**

Glechoma hederacea
Gk *glechon*, mint or thyme
L *hederacea*, ivy-like

A creeping perennial with erect flowering stems. Long-stalked, opposite, kidney-shaped, bluntly toothed leaves on both creeping and flowering stems. Slightly aromatic. Flowers in whorls of 2 or 4 up stem all face same way, violet blue, 2 notched lips on straight tube. Fruits 4 nutlets. Astringent, diuretic. Infusions used for haemorrhoids, coughs, catarrh and abdominal disorders. A gargle for mouth and throat infections. A tonic and vermifuge. Before the introduction of hops in sixteenth century used for flavouring beer, hence name Alehoof. Young shoots and leaves added to soup or used like spinach.

HOREHOUND, BLACK

STINKING ROGER, MADWORT

Height 30–130 cm/12–51 in ❀ **June–September**

Ballota nigra
Gk *ballo*, reject, throw away
L *nigra*, dark or black

A hairy straggling perennial superficially like Red Dead-nettle, with opposite, toothed, short-stalked ovate leaves, smelling strongly of nettles. Lilac 2-lipped flowers are borne in whorls up the leafy stems. Grows on hedge banks, waysides and waste ground. Culpeper recommended it for consumption, coughs, phlegm, pains in the sides and some gynaecological conditions, as well as for treating bites from mad dogs. It was thought to be less effective than Common Horehound.

HOUND'S-TONGUE

Height 30–90 cm/12–36 in ❀ May–August

Cynoglossum officinale
Gk *kuon*, dog; Gk *glosso*, tongue (leaf shape)
L *officinale*, used by apothecaries for medicinal
purposes

A greyish hairy perennial of dry, grassy places
often on lime. A branched, fleshy rootstock
rears erect stems with untoothed, lance-
shaped, greyish, alternate leaves with soft
hairs. Maroon-red, 5-petalled, funnel-shaped
flowers held in loose spikes. A hairy cup with
hooked spines bears 4 nutlets. The whole
plant smells of mouse, or roasted peanut.
Culpeper said leaves cured mad dog bites,
falling hair, burns and scalds; roots helped
lung and blood conditions, or it was baked
into suppositories for piles. Used in proprietary
medicines for piles, phlebitis, eczema, mastitis,
haematoma and gastritis. Young shoots eaten
like asparagus, young leaves as a vegetable or
in soups and stews.

IRIS, STINKING

ROAST BEEF PLANT, GLADDON,
DRAGON'S TONGUE, BLUE DEVIL

Height 30–60 cm/12–24 in ❀ June–July

Iris foetidissima
Iris, Gk goddess of the rainbow
L *foetidissima*, stinking

Thick tufts of dark evergreen sword-like leaves
rise from perennial rhizomes. The leaves are
fetid when crushed, hence name. 1–5 short-
lived smallish flowers are held on an upright
stem. Slatey-violet flowers sometimes tinged
yellow, falls faintly veined. Orange seeds in
3-part capsule. Favours chalky soil. To many
people the adjective 'fetid' is not appropriate;
the odour of the bruised leaves being more
reminiscent of roast beef – hence its
vernacular name.

KNAPWEED, COMMON

BLACK KNAPWEED, HORSEKNOPS,
PAINTBRUSH

Height 30–60 cm/12–24 in ❀ June–September

Centaurea nigra
In Gk mythology, Chiron, wisest of the
centaurs, used it for its healing powers
L *nigra*, black (patterning on calyx)

A downy perennial with stiff ribbed stems.
Lower leaves are lance-shaped with short
teeth and long stalks, upper leaves neither
toothed nor stalked. Solitary or small clusters
of crowded purple flowers in a globular,
thistle-like cup with blackish, bristly bracts are
held erect at stem tops. Seeds have short hairs
on top. Grows in coarse grass and roadsides.
Used for wounds, ruptures, bruises, scabs, sore
throats, and for rubbing on cows' udders after
calving. Maidens foretold their marriage
prospects by pulling off the outer florets and
placing the rest of the flower in their blouse.

KNAPWEED, GREATER

Height up to 120 cm/45 in ❀ July–September

Centaurea scabiosa
In Gk mythology, Chiron, wisest of the
centaurs, used it for its healing powers
From L *scabius*, scabies (which it was used
to treat)

An upright perennial with erect stout bristly
stems, swollen at the top, bearing alternate
pinnately lobed leaves, the lower ones stalked.
Large terminal flower heads with purple florets
above green bracts (like a thistle top). The
sterile, rayed outer florets form a crown.
Grassy places, especially on lime. Species
name reveals one medicinal use. Like related
Cornflower, it is an astringent for reducing
inflammation, and used externally it is helpful
in the treatment of minor wounds. Culpeper
noted: 'it is good for those bruised by any falls
or blows, by drinking a decoction of the herb
roots in wine and applying the same outwardly
to the place'. Florets used fresh in salads.

LUCERNE

ALFALFA, MEDICK, PURPLE MEDICLE

Height 30–60 cm/12–24 in ❀ June–October

Medicago sativa
L *medica* from Gk *medike*, (grass) of the Medes
or ancient Persians
L *sativa*, cultivated; Lucerne from L *lucerna*,
light (with reference to its shiny seeds)

An erect or sprawling hairy perennial with
short-stalked partly toothed trefoil leaves and
clustered spikes of blue to violet pea-flowers.
Seeds in a spiralled pod. Grassy and waste
places. Used as a healing herb by Chinese as
beverage cure for stomach ulcers. Also used
medicinally for anaemia, haemorrhoids,
gynaecological complaints and hormonal
imbalance. Grown as a fodder plant since
it was introduced by King Darius of Persia
(521–486 BC). Nitrogen-enriching for soil
and good for milk yield. Lucerne sprouts useful
in salad, with a taste like fresh peas. Rich in
vitamins and proteins.

MADDER, FIELD

Prostrate ❀ May–September

Sherardia arvensis
L *sherardia* after William Sherard (1659–1728)
who endowed the Chair of Botany at Oxford
L *arvensis*, of cultivated fields

A much-branched prostrate annual bearing
whorls of 4–6 short fat hairy leaves. Minute
lilac-pink 4-petalled flowers with long corolla
tubes borne in dense terminal clusters. Seeds
round and bristly. A typical Bedstraw, it
is usually pollinated by flies. Related to
Squinancywort. Red dye was extracted
from the slender, coloured roots and used
to colour cloth but it was not as brilliant as
that extracted from the true Madder (*Rubia
tinctorum*).

MARJORAM

WILD MARJORAM

Height 20–40 cm/12–24 in   ❀ July–September

Origanum vulgare
Gk *oros*, mountain; Gk *ganos*, joy
L *vulgare*, common or wild

A tufted hairy perennial with branching
upright stems. Short-stalked, oval to lance-
shaped leaves in opposite pairs. Small
bunched heads of 2-lipped purplish flowers
borne above purplish bracts. The flowers have
a notched upper, and a 3-lobed lower lip.
Fruits are 4 nutlets in a cup of short pointed
sepals. Contains a volatile oil, is antibacterial
and antifungal. Antiseptic. Essences are good
for coughs and breathing problems. Marjoram
Tea helps indigestion, ear-ache, coughs, dropsy
and bladder troubles. Diluted oil can be
rubbed into aching teeth and joints. Perfume
used in cosmetics. Symbolises happiness –
young couples were garlanded with Marjoram
in ancient Greece and Rome.

MINT, WATER

HORSEMINT (N. England)

Height 15–60 cm/6–24 in   ❀ July–September

Mentha aquatica
L *mentha*, mint; L *aquatica*, of water

A perennial with a creeping, frequently
rooting, slender rootstock. Stiff often reddish
stems bear pairs of opposite, short-stalked,
pointed-oval, toothed, hairy leaves. Dense
clusters or whorls of lilac-coloured flowers
occur at base of upper leaves. A strewing herb.
Ancient Greeks used it in bath water, also
used in fourteenth- and fifteenth-century
Britain for its cleansing, refreshing, masking
properties. Used for diarrhoea and menstrual
discharges. Mint Tea aids digestion and, taken
hot, induces perspiration in heavy cold
sufferers. Still used pharmaceutically to flavour
gargles and mouthwashes, and for flavouring
drinks.

ORCHID, COMMON SPOTTED

PRIEST, SNAKE'S FLOWER, SATYRION,
FINGER ORCHIS

Height 15–60 cm/6–24 in   ❀ Late May–early August

Dactylorhiza fuchsii
Gk *dactylos*, finger; Gk *rhiza*, root
Fuchsii after German botanist Leonhart Fuchs
(1501–66). Gerard refers to its Latin name
'Palma Christi' after the shape of its tubers

Old tuber has 4 tapering fingers, new tuber
is sac-like. Lowest leaves broad oval, upper
leaves narrower, spotted and pointed, up
to 8. Flower spike up to 5 inches long, flowers
variable in colour from white to pale/dark
purple with darker purple spots. White form
may not have petal spots. Upper sepals and
petals form a hood, lateral sepals spread like
wings. Broad lip has 3 triangular lobes, marked
with looped lines or spots. Pollinated by bees
and flies. Found in all kinds of soil.

ORCHID, SOUTHERN MARSH

COMMON MARSH ORCHID

Height up to 76 cm/30 in   ❀ May–July

Dactylorhiza praetermissa
Gk *dactylos*, finger; Gk *rhiza*, root
L *praetermissa*, overlooked, neglected

Underground tubers bear hollow aerial shoots
of up to 45 cm/18 in with 5–9 greyish-green
fat, ribbed, pointed, lance-shaped leaves,
usually unspotted and a dense cylindrical spike
of dark or rose-pink flowers, with a dark-
spotted saucer-like lip, spur stout and curved
with a blunt tip, the sepals spread out and
upwards. Pointed leaf-like bracts below each
flower. A short, curved, blunt spur. Most
abundant marsh orchid in S. England. Likes
wet places including damp meadows in chalky
or limestone areas.

PASQUE FLOWER

Height up to 30 cm/13 in ❀ April–May

Pulsatilla vulgaris
L *pulsare*, to beat or sway (as in the wind)
L *vulgaris*, common

A low, hairy perennial that produces a single flower before the leaves appear. The large flowers are erect at first, then drooping, with 6 rich violet, sometimes reddish petals (in fact sepals) covered with silky hairs on the back eventually above a whorl of feathery leaves. Flower has a centre of golden stamens of which the inner rings provide pollen, the outer rings nectar. The true basal leaves are pinnately divided into a fan. Small seeds have feathery plumes, often persisting well into summer. A rare chalk grassland plant that flowers around Easter, hence name. Several flower regularly on the Barton Hills (Walk 18B). A remedy for cramping pain, menstrual and eye problems. One of the most commonly used of all homeopathic remedies.

PURPLE-LOOSESTRIFE

RED SALLY

Height 60–120 cm/24–48 in ❀ June–August

Lythrum salicaria
Gk *luthron*, gore, blood from an injury (reference to the flower's vivid colour)
L *salicaria*, willow-like
Sally from L *salix*, willow

An erect perennial with a stout 4-sided hairy stem. Lower leaves, unstalked, in whorls of 3; upper leaves untoothed, lance-shaped, in opposite pairs. Flowers are borne in whorls of 6 above small leaf-like bracts; reddish-purple, 6-petalled, and forming slender spikes at stem top. Oval capsule bears seeds. Water margins. Culpeper recommended it for eye complaints, inter-menstrual bleeding and as a wound poultice. In Ireland an infusion was used for diarrhoea and dysentery. Juice, rich in tannins, is an alternative to oak bark for tanning leather.

SCABIOUS, DEVIL'S-BIT

Height 15–100 cm/6–40 in   July–September

Succisa pratensis
L *succisa*, abruptly broken off, pruned
L *pratensis*, of meadows

A perennial herb with a short upright root,
abruptly ended as if bitten off (allegedly by the
Devil, furious at its success as a cure-all, but
failing to destroy its curative properties). A
rosette of stalked elliptical leaves, sometimes
purplish, supports slender, hairy, upright stems
with narrower, sometimes toothed, opposite
leaves. At the top it carries one largish
hemispherical head of tightly packed lilac to
dark blue funnel-shaped florets, with smaller
flowers rising below on slender stalks from leaf
bract joints on either side of the stem. Damp
grassy places on acid soil or lime. Culpeper
prescribed boiled root for snakebite, swollen
throats, wounds, plague and shortness of
breath. Still used for coughs, fevers, internal
inflammation, and to remove dandruff.

SCABIOUS, FIELD

MEADOW SCABIOUS, LADY'S PIN CUSHION

Height 25–100 cm/10–40 in   June–October

Knautia arvensis
Named after Dr Knaut (1654–1716), a
botanist from Saxony
L *arvensis*, of cultivated fields

A medium to tall hairy perennial with
notched, undivided lance-shaped basal leaves,
its upper leaves much divided like a fish-bone
and hairy. Blue-mauve flowers held in a pin
cushion of up to 50 florets, the outer ones
larger and rayed. Seeds crowned with bristles
and 16 tiny purple sepals. Dry grassy places,
avoiding heavy soils. A long-used source of
cures for scabies (hence its common name),
other skin diseases, and plague. Infusions
taken for purifying the blood, applying to
cuts, burns and bruises. Decoction or ointment
made from roots cured sores, eruptions
and other skin defects. Gypsies used it to
strengthen the lungs and against pleurisy.

SELFHEAL

CARPENTERS' HERB, HOOK HEAL,
SICKLY WORT

Height 5–30 cm/2–12 in ❀ June–October

Prunella vulgaris
From L *prunum*, purple, or Ger *Braune*, quinsy
(for which it is a cure)
L *vulgaris*, common

Low patch-forming hairy perennial, producing
erect flowering stems with slightly toothed
oval pointed leaves. Purple 2-lipped flowers
resting on spreading pointed bracts are set in
regular tiers in a tight whorl at the top of stem
above a pair of stalkless leaves. Fruit consists
of 4 small nutlets from each flower. Upper lip
of flower hook-shaped, so plant invoked
according to Doctrine of Signatures to cure
wounds (made by sickles or bill-hooks). Used
by Greeks to cure sore throats and tonsillitis.
Can help lower blood pressure and is effective
antibiotic against the sources of urinary
infections and enteritis. Used in spring salads.

TEASEL, WILD

VENUS' BASIN, BRUSHES AND COMBS,
JOHNNY-PRICK-THE-FINGER

Height up to 200 cm/80 in ❀ July–September

Dipsacus fullonum
Gk *dipsa*, thirst (from the way rainwater
collects in cups at base of leaves); L *fullonum*,
of cloth-fullers (who used it to comb out wool)

A tall, hairless, upright biennial with stout
stems, prickly on the angles, with a basal
rosette of rough, short-lived oblong leaves,
and narrower broad lance-shaped stem leaves,
cupped at the base. From the axils globular
buds grow into spiny ovoid tight clusters
of flowers that open 2 or 3 rows at a time,
cradled by long ascending spiny bracts. Roots
used for stomach ailments. Not much used by
herbalists. Insects can become trapped and
drown in water that collects at the base of the
leaves. Their bodies, broken down by bacteria,
may release extra nutrients for the plant.

THISTLE, DWARF

GROUND THISTLE, DWARF MAY THISTLE

Height 5–15 cm/2–6 in ✿ June–September

Cirsium acaule
Gk *kirsos*, swollen vein (for which it is a
remedy); L *acaule*, stemless

A low perennial with a long woody rootstock.
Basal rosette of spiny, rigid, wavily cut
stemless leaves from which rises a solitary
flower of purple florets on an ovoid globe of
purple-tipped flower bracts. Seeds on small
'parachutes' for wind dispersal. Grows in
short turf on chalk or limestone, mainly in
S. England. Harmful on pastures because it
kills all plants beneath it. The root was once
chewed to alleviate toothache and swollen
veins.

THISTLE, MUSK

NODDING THISTLE

Height 30–90 cm/12–36 in ✿ June–September

Carduus nutans
L *carduus*, thistle; L *nutans*, drooping, nodding

A biennial thistle with cottony, downy stems,
winged below, with long, deeply cut leaves
with spines on the lobes. Upper drooping
spine-free stems bear large fragrant, reddish-
purple, nodding flower-heads. The bracts
surrounding the flower heads have spiny
down-curved tips. A most attractive thistle
growing in open grassland on chalk and
limestone. Culpeper suggests no medical
or culinary uses. The down may be used in
paper-making.

THYME, WILD

Height 5–10 cm/2–4 in ✤ May–September

Thymus polytrichus
Gk *thumon* from Gk *thuein*, to burn or sacrifice (Theophrastus' name for a plant used in sacrificial rites); L *polytrichus*, hairy

A creeping mat-forming perennial with woody runners. Short square stems have hairs on 2 opposite sides. Short-stalked opposite leathery leaves, oval with long bristles around edges and oil glands on upper surfaces. Undersides veined. Flowers red-purple in round terminal heads. Highly perfumed, long lasting, it was used as a strewing herb. Antiseptic, it is taken for throat and digestive illnesses, laryngitis and whooping cough. An infusion rubbed into scalp allegedly retains hair colour. Its extract, Glycerine of Thymol, is used in patent medicines. Favourite flower of fairies; sometimes planted on graves. Also used in cooking with lamb or in bouquet garni, also in herb butter, herb vinegar.

TOADFLAX, PALE

Height 30–60 cm/12–24 in ✤ June–September

Linaria repens
L *linaria*, flax-like; L *repens*, creeping (stolons)

A grey hairless perennial with creeping stem that produces further upright stems. Slim round branching stems bear whorls of linear one-veined leaves, then branching flower spikes with loose bunches of pale lilac snapdragon-like flowers, the lip veined purple. They also have a purple-veined spur with an orange spot on the bulge. Dry, rather bare grassy and waste places. A naturalised European plant that hybridises with native Common and Purple Toadflax where they grow together. Vernacular name refers to likeness of the flowers to the wide mouth of a toad.

VERVAIN

HERB OF GRACE

Height up to 75 cm/30 in ❀ **June–September**

Verbena officinalis
L *verbena*, leaves or twigs of sacred plants,
used in religious ceremonies; L *officinalis*,
used by apothecaries for medicinal purposes
Celt *ferfaen*, drive away stone (referring to
use in bladder infections)

A rough hairy perennial with tough square
stems with pinnately lobed, diamond-shaped
opposite leaves. Small pale pink to lilac 5-
petalled flowers rise up a slim leafless spike.
It grows in scrub and wasteland, especially
on chalk or limestone. Herbalists used it to
treat depression, nervous tension, asthma,
jaundice, headaches and minor skin problems.
According to legend, Vervain grew on Calvary
and was used to staunch Christ's blood at the
Crucifixion. Worn round the head it was
believed to be a talisman against headaches
and poisonous bites.

VETCH, BUSH

Height 30–100 cm/12–40 in ❀ **April–October**

Vicia sepium
L *vicia*, vetch; L *vincire*, to bind (referring to
the tendrils); L *sepium*, of hedgerows

A hairy scrambling perennial. Ridged stems
bear downy leaves of 5–8 pairs of ovate leaflets
with terminal points, the whole leaf tipped
with branching support-seeking tendrils. Dull
purple fading to blue pea flowers are borne in
clusters of 2–6. Seeds held in hairless pods
tapering to a beak turn black before seeds are
ejected. Widespread in hedges and scrub, and
very attractive to bumble bees. Called 'bush'
not because it is one, but because it scrambles
for support up through shrubs and other
plants. Although related to the Broad Bean it
has no culinary use, but was once fed to cattle.

VETCH, COMMON

Height 15–120 cm/12–48 in ✿ May–September

Vicia sativa
L *vincire*, to bind (referring to the tendrils)
L *sativa*, cultivated

A slightly hairy scrambling annual. Straggly
stems bear leaves with 4–8 opposite pairs of
lance-shaped leaflets and a tendril, often
branched, at the tips. Reddish purple pea
flowers, solitary or in pairs, borne on short
stalks up the stem, their wings of a darker
purple. Smooth pods bearing 4–12 seeds have
a long beak. Grassy and waste places. Despite
its name, not the most abundant of British
vetches, common only in S.E. England.
A fodder crop introduced in ancient times
from Western Asia.

VETCH, TUFTED

FINGERS AND THUMBS (Somerset)

Height 60–200 cm/24–80 in ✿ June–September

Vicia cracca
L *vincire*, to bind (referring to the tendrils)
L *cracca*, name used by Pliny for a species of
vetch growing in cereal crops

A downy clambering perennial of hedge,
scrub, pasture and woodland edge. Ridged
stems bear leaves of 12–24 opposite, lance-
shaped leaflets with a tendril at the tip. Spikes
of up to 40 blue-purple pea flowers hang one-
sided on long erect stalks. Smooth brown pods
contain seeds. Pods end in a nail or claw,
giving name Fingers and Thumbs. No known
domestic use except as animal fodder.

VIOLET, EARLY DOG

Height 2.5–20 cm/1–8 in ❀ **March–May**

Viola reichenbachiana
L *viola*, plant family name; *reichenbachiana*
after botanist Heinrich Gustav Reichenbach
(1823–89); dog, suggesting its inferiority to
other varieties as it has no scent

A low rather hairy perennial with lateral leafy
flowering stems and basal leaf rosettes. Heart-
shaped leaves as broad as long and with
serrated edges. Scentless violet-blue flowers
generally darker in the centre with a slender
straight dark violet-blue spur, not notched or
furrowed. Fruit a triangular 3-valved seed
capsule. Dog Violet is cathartic and emetic but
not much used now. An infusion of violet can
be used for headaches. Gypsies make a
poultice from the leaves to treat cancers.
Common Dog Violet (*Viola riviniana*) has
deeper violet-blue flowers with a stout whitish
or pale purple spur, often upcurved and
generally blooming a month later.

VIOLET, SWEET

Height up to 15 cm/6 in ❀ **February–May**

Viola odorata
L *viola*, plant family name; L *odorata*, scented

A long rhizome with rooting stolons (like a
strawberry) supports a rosette of notched,
long-stalked, heart-shaped, finely toothed
leaves. Slim flower-stalks rise to support
single, scented, deep violet or white flowers
with 2 erect and 3 spurred pendulant lower
petals. Blunt sepals. Seeds in a 3-valved hairy
capsule. Used medicinally for bronchitis,
coughs, asthma, some cancers, throat
infections and skin problems. Essential oil is
used in perfumery. Flowers used fresh in salads
and candied for cake ornament or flavouring.
Hairy Violet (*Viola hirta*) is found on Walks 11
and 19. It differs from Sweet Violet in having
no runners, no fragrance and a paler, bluer
violet colour as well as being hairier.

WOUNDWORT, HEDGE

ALL-HEAL, CLOWN'S WOUNDWORT

Height 30–90 cm/12–36 in ✱ June–October

Stachys sylvatica
Gk *stakhus*, ear of wheat, spike
L *sylvatica*, of woods

A strong-smelling creeping perennial. Hairy upright many-branched stems bear long-stalked, toothed, hairy heart-shaped leaves in opposite pairs. Loose spikes of flowers are borne in whorls, dark red-purple with tiny bracts below. Upper petals form hoods, lower have a white marked lobed lip. Hairy sepal tube holds seeds. Effective in staunching wounds and applied as a poultice to remove warts and swellings around the head. The distilled juices of the flowers were used 'to make the heart merry, to make a good colour in the face, and make the vitall spirits more fresh and lively'. It produces a yellow dye. Eaten by sheep and goats, but shunned by cattle and pigs.

WOUNDWORT, MARSH

CLOWN'S WOUNDWORT, ALL-HEAL

Height 40–100 cm/16–40 in ✱ late June–September

Stachys palustris
Gk *stakhus*, ear of wheat, spike
L *palustris*, of marshy places

A hairy perennial with stout, spreading, fleshy, underground stolons which throw up erect, four-sided flower stems bearing short-stalked, hairy, toothed, lance-shaped leaves in opposite pairs. Whorls of pale purple, spotted with dark purple, snapdragon-like flowers are spaced above small unstalked leaves up the spike. Gerard relates how he met a labourer with a scythe wound to the leg, right down to the bone. He dressed the bleeding wound himself with leaves of this plant, and within a week it was healed, hence Clown's Woundwort. Used to relieve gout, cramp and vertigo. Young shoots can be eaten as asparagus, as also the tubers collected in autumn.

BALSAM, HIMALAYAN

INDIAN BALSAM, POLICEMAN'S HELMET,
NUNS, JUMPING JACK

Height 100–200 cm/40–80 in ❀ June–October

Impatiens glandulifera
L *impatiens*, impatient (denoting explosive
seed release); L *glandulifera*, with glands

A fragile annual with ribbed, often reddish
stems. Leaves are in whorls of 3, pointed
and edged with short red teeth. Large pink-
purple flowers are held on individual stalks in
small groups, spotted inside and with a strong
scent, the common name Policeman's Helmet
being a good description. Seeds are borne
in exploding narrow club-shaped capsules.
Our tallest and commonest balsam, it was
introduced in 1839, an aggressive coloniser of
waterside, banks and waste ground. Medicinal
use (if any) unknown, but in the Far East an
extract is used as a nail varnish.

BARTSIA, RED

Height up to 50 cm/20 in ❀ June–September

Odontites vernus
From Gk *odous, odontos*, tooth (used for
treating toothache); L *vernus*, of springtime
Bartsia, after Dr Bartoch, named by Swedish
botanist Linnaeus after a close friend

A hairy purplish annual, upright stems, usually
branched below, have toothed, lance-shaped,
opposite, reddish-green leaves at the upper
ends of the stems. Small, pink-purple, two-
lipped flowers, the lower lip 3-lobed, grow on
very short stalks from one side to form a loose
spike. Single seeds fill the calyx. A plant of
cornfields, waste spaces and roadsides. This
plant is semi-parasitic, extracting water and
minerals from the roots of adjacent grasses.
Once considered a cure for toothache.

CAMPION, RED

BACHELORS' BUTTONS, MOTHER DIE

Height 30–90 cm/12–36 in   🌸 **March–October**

Silene dioica
Gk *silene* from Gk *sialon*, saliva (gummy exudation on stems) or from Silenus, the intoxicated foster-father of Bacchus
Gk *dioica*, two dwellings (male stamens and female pistils on separate plants)

A hardy perennial with a creeping stock, often in clumps. Hairy very upright flowering stems bear pointed oval leaves, stalked at base, unstalked and opposite up the stem. Deeply divided bright rosy-pink 5-petalled flowers are unscented. Sepals are joined to form a sticky tube. Fruits in capsules with 10 teeth rolled back when ripe. Culpeper used it for kidney stoppages, stones, internal bleeding, cleaning old sores and wounds, and in wine against scorpion stings, snakebites and plague. In Wales, a plant associated with snakes, the Devil, goblins and death.

CENTAURY, COMMON

BANWORT, BLOODWORT

Height 2–50 cm/1–20 in   🌸 **June–October**

Centaurium erythraea
The centaur Chiron was healed by this plant from a wound inflicted by the 9-headed Hydra
Gk *erythros*, red

A hairless annual with a basal rosette of pointed oval leaves and a few opposite pairs up stem slightly smaller and veined. Unstalked pink flowers in terminal clusters on short branches. Gentian-like flower has 5 narrow keeled teeth. Fruit capsule longer than calyx. Grows in grassy places. Used for arthritis, anaemia, gall and liver ailments, indigestion, anorexia, hiatus hernia and fevers. Culpeper said it removed freckles. A lotion applied to the skin was supposed to deter fleas and lice. Chaucer's 'Nun's Priest's Tale' relates its use as a laxative.

CORALROOT

CORALROOT BITTERCRESS

Height 35–70 cm/14–28 in ❀ April–May

Cardamine bulbifera
Gk *kardamon*, cress; L *bulbifera*, producing
bulbs

A creeping perennial rhizome gives rise to
a number of erect slender unbranched stems
with no basal rosette but with toothed lance-
shaped pinnate leaves below; upper leaves
simple with bulbils developing in the axils.
4-petalled pinkish lilac flowers clustered on
short stalks at head. Seed pods seldom ripen,
but propagation takes place with bulbils. Like
a taller more rigid Lady's Smock. Grows in
calcareous woods or damp places. A speciality
of the Chilterns and the eastern Weald.

CRANE'S-BILL, CUT-LEAVED

Height 10–30 cm/4–12 in ❀ April–September

Geranium dissectum
Gk *geranos*, crane (bill-like fruit)
L *dissectum*, deeply divided (leaves)

A coarse, often reddish downy annual. Hairy
upright or sprawling stems bear finger-like
leaves jaggedly cut almost to base. Short-
stalked flowers have notched purplish-pink
petals and very hairy sepals with a bristle
on the tips. Downy fruits hold 4 pitted seeds.
These details differentiate it from the rarer
Long-Stalked Crane's-bill (*Geranium
columbinum*). Used medicinally as a styptic,
astringent and tonic. Taken internally for
diarrhoea, cholera and chronic dysentery.
A useful gargle. Possibly used by early
herbalists as a cure for ruptures. This plant
occurs mainly on disturbed or waste land,
road verges and quarries.

CRANE'S-BILL, DOVE'S-FOOT
MOTHER OF MILLIONS

Height 8–20 cm/3–8 in   ❀ April–September

Geranium molle
Gk *geranos*, crane (bill-like fruit); L *molle*, soft

Prostrate hairy annual with rounded lobed leaves. Lower leaves have long stalks, upper short-stalked. Five notched pink-lilac to purple petals and 5 hairy pointed sepals. Seeds in wrinkled case that opens when ripe to eject a seed from each style. Leaf supposed to resemble a dove's foot, seed pod a crane's beak. Culpeper used it for colic, gallstones, inward bleeding, gout or joint ache. Gerard recommended the powdered plant in red wine as a miraculous cure of ruptures and burstings, with the proviso that 'in aged persons it shall be needful to adde thereto the powder of red snails (those without shells), dried in an oven, in number nine . . . that never faileth'.

CRANE'S-BILL, HEDGEROW
PYRENEAN CRANE'S-BILL,
MOUNTAIN CRANE'S-BILL

Height 22–45 cm/9–18 in   ❀ May–September

Geranium pyrenaicum
Gk *geranos*, a crane (bill-like fruit)
L *pyrenaicum*, from the Pyrenees

A hairy perennial with short-stalked roundish leaves with 5–7 wedge-shaped lobes. Pairs of pinkish-purple flowers with deeply notched petals and narrow pointed sepals develop the typical crane's bill-like seed pods. A common plant of wayside and hedgerow in S. and E. England. Not recorded here until 1762.

CUCKOOFLOWER

LADY'S SMOCK, MILKMAID

Height 15–60 cm/6–24 in ❀ March–June

Cardamis pratensis
Gk *kardamon*, cress; L *pratensis*, of meadows

A hairless perennial of damp places. A rosette of basal leaves, pinnate with a larger terminal leaflet, upper leaves narrower. Flowers in a loose bunch held high. Four notched petals, lilac to white with deep lilac veins. Anthers yellow. Seed pods erect like small cucumbers. Often forms broad colonies in damp spots. Infusions used against scurvy, dropsy, epileptic fits and skin ailments. Folk superstition associates picking this plant with adder bites (Austria), lightning strike (Germany) or bad luck (England), especially if brought into the home. Young leaves, shoots and buds in salad taste like watercress.

FUMITORY

Height 15–50 cm/6–20 in ❀ April–October

Fumaria officinalis
L *fumare*, to smoke (effect of juice on eyes like that of smoke); L *officinalis*, used by apothecaries for medicinal purposes
Fumitory from L *fumus terrae*, smoke of the earth

A robust hairless scrambling annual. Deeply cut pinnate leaves have slender bluish-green leaflets. Erect spikes bear many flowers, tubular with a short spur, waisted, pinkish-purple tipped maroon. Small single globular seeds on short stalks succeed up the stem. Pull a root to release a gaseous smell like nitric acid. Common in waste places where it can look smoky from a distance. Long used in Europe and beyond as a diuretic, a gentle laxative, a detoxifier, to treat liver, gall-bladder and skin conditions, and as a lotion to cleanse flaking skin and pimples. Still used in a number of proprietary medicines.

HEMP-AGRIMONY

ANDURION, HOLY ROPE

Height 30–120 cm/12–48 in ❀ July–September

Eupatorium cannabinum
Eupatorium after Mithridates Eupator, King of
Pontus; L *cannabinum*, resembling cannabis
(leaflets)

A tall downy perennial with a woody
rootstock. Round reddish downy furrowed
stem with few short branches, aromatic smell
when cut. Coarsely toothed leaves, leaflets
palmately lobed and short stalked are borne
in opposite pairs up stem. Dense clusters
of reddish-pink flowers at end of branches.
Seeds have parachutes of white hairs. Early
herbalists used it for many cures. Used as a
purge, emetic, a cure for dropsy and jaundice.
As a poultice, or mixed with lard as an
ointment, healed wounds. As an infusion it
helped colds and flu, but had to be used with
caution. Leaves laid on bread stopped it
becoming mouldy.

HERB-ROBERT

STINKING BOB, DEATH COME QUICKLY

Height 10–50 cm/4–20 in ❀ April–October

Geranium robertianum
Gk *geranos*, crane (bill-like fruit)
Species name from corrupted L *ruber*, red, or
after St Robert of Salzburg (Ruprecht), our
Robin Goodfellow

Strong-smelling hairy annual, often reddish,
especially on stems. Triangular fern-like
leaves in 3–5 segments. Pink flowers have
5 rounded unnotched petals. Fruit slightly
wrinkled shaped like a crane's beak, seeds
attached until ripe to a slim filament are
smooth. Finches love the seeds. Strong
putrid smell attractive to insect pollinators.
By the Doctrine of Signatures, redness implied
cure for blood disorders or stemming blood
flow. Herbal uses include diarrhoea, dropsy,
gum inflammation and mouth bleeding.
Associated with snakes and headaches.

MALLOW, COMMON

BILLY BUTTONS, PANCAKE PLANT,
CHEESE CAKES

Height 30–90 cm/12–36 in ❀ June–September

Malva sylvestris
L *malva*, soft; L *sylvestris*, of woodland
Common name from Gk *malassein*, to soften

An erect to sprawling perennial. A thick,
erect hairy stem bears kidney- to rounded-
shaped lobed toothed leaves. Large 2.5–5 cm/
1–2 in rose-pink flowers borne in clusters
have 5 narrow notched dark-veined petals.
Rounded fruits ('cheeses') contain netted
nutlet seeds. Reputed as an anti-aphrodisiac,
promoting calm, sober conduct. White root
used in treatment of gravel, irritations of the
kidneys and, ground into a poultice and
applied hot, for wasp and bee stings or
inflammation. Pliny advocated crushing
leaves with nitre to draw out thorns and
prickles. Young shoots were eaten as vegetable
in Roman times.

MUSK-MALLOW

Height 30–120 cm/12–48 in ❀ June–August

Malva moschata
L *malva*, soft; L *moschata*, musky
Common name from Gk *malassein*, to soften

An erect perennial with a round thick stem
covered with purplish hairs and bearing finely
divided lobed leaves. Large 5-petalled rose-
coloured flowers with darker veins form loose
clusters towards the top of the stem. Seeds
held in hairy seed cases. This plant is
widespread in grassy places and open scrub
throughout S. England. When crushed the
leaves emit a musky fragrance. The white
roots and the leaves are not as effective as
Common Mallow, and so were seldom used
pharmaceutically.

ORCHID, BEE

Height 15–60 cm/6–24 in ❀ June–July

Ophrys apifera
Gk *ophrys*, eyebrow (indication of high regard, or referring to furry edges of lips)
L *apifera*, bee-bearing

A widespread British orchid, which grows from 2 globular tubers. A single flower stem bears oval grey-green leaves that persist all winter, wrapped round the stem, with narrower leaves above. 2–7 widely spaced flowers mimic bumble bees to encourage pollination. Spreading, large green-veined pink petals surround smaller curled up green petals. The lip is bag-shaped, red or purplish-brown, softly hairy with a red-brown throat. It has side lobes like small hairy cones behind the lip. Grasslands on lime. Varies enormously in numbers from year to year. Culpeper says that roots were used to provoke lust, to kill worms in children and to aid conception. Starchy roots eaten during famine.

ORCHID, FRAGRANT

SCENTED ORCHID, CLOVE ORCHID

Height 15–45 cm/6–18 in ❀ June–July

Gymnadenia conopsea
Gk *gymnos*, naked; Gk *aden*, gland
Gk *conopsea*, cone-shaped (tubers)

Double parsnip-like tubers are infected by mycorhiza to aid nourishment. Aerial stem, rising 3 years after germination, has 3–5 long narrow erect leaves on lower stem, a few smaller ones further up. Dense flower head of pink flowers. 3-lobed lip has a long slender spur. Upper sepals and petals form a hood. Strong vanilla scent attracts pollinating insects. 50–90 per cent successful pollination. Grows in short turf or on lime. Numbers can fluctuate dramatically from year to year, apparently due to periodic failure of seedlings to establish themselves. Any pharmaceutical uses obscure.

ORCHID, LADY

Height 20–40 cm/8–16 in   ❀ May–June

Orchis purpurea
L *orkhis*, testicle (referring to shape of tuber)
L *purpurea*, reddish-purple

An outsize version of the Burnt-tip Orchid.
3–5 shiny broad basal leaves cradle the tall
stem that supports a crowded spike of fragrant
flowers. Dark purplish-brown hooded sepals
above pale pink lip. Each flower gives the
appearance of a lady – a brownish-purple
head above dotted pale pink arms and skirt.
The ovary is a short, curved spur pointing
downwards. A rare orchid that grows on
chalk, mainly in Kent, but is also present
in the Chilterns (Walk 3).

ORCHID, MILITARY

SOLDIER ORCHID

Height 15–45 cm/6–18 in   ❀ May–June

Orchis militaris
L *orkhis*, testicle (referring to shape of tuber)
L *militaris*, like a soldier

This rare and declining orchid's aerial stem
develops in the fourth year, the flower spike
some years later. It bears 4 or 5 broad, blunt
leaves at the base, 1 or 2 smaller higher up.
The sepal hood (soldier's helmet) is white
or pale pink, the hanging pink 4-lobed lip
spotted dark pink. It bears a short down-
curved spur. Once used like many other
orchids for the preparation of 'salep', a
nutritious tonic beverage sold at London
street stalls before coffee replaced it. Once
widespread in S. Britain, especially in the
Chilterns, now only on three sites – two in
the Chilterns (Walk 7), one in W. Suffolk.

ORCHID, MONKEY

Height 15–30 cm/6–12 in ❀ May–June

Orchis simia
L *orkhis*, testicle (referring to shape of tuber)
L *simia*, monkey-shaped

Two egg-shaped tubers and few fleshy roots develop 4 years after germination, then a small leaf for several years before the aerial root emerges. The stem has 2 broad blunt leaves at the base, and 2 or 3 narrower ones almost encircling the stem higher up. The short dense flower spike has 20 or more flowers, unusually the top ones opening first. The greyish white hood is faintly spotted or streaked with purple; the monkey-like 'body' is red-spotted pale pinkish, the slim 'legs' curving downwards. It has a short blunt spur at the base of the lip. Growing on chalk hills, it is now rare; with one site in the Chilterns (Walk 3), and two in Kent.

ORCHID, PYRAMIDAL

Height 20–45 cm/8–18 in ❀ June–August

Anacamptis pyramidalis
Gk *anakamptein*, to bend backwards (the long spur); L *pyramidalis*, pyramidal

Two round tubers develop from seed over 4 years aided by fungus. Leaves appear after 5 years, flowers several years later. Longish fleshy lower leaves, narrow lance-shaped upper, hug stem alternately. Unspotted. Pyramid of pink flowers at first, later cylindrical. Short upper petals and sepals form hood, deep 3-lobed lip slopes forward and down. Long slender spur, same length as ovary. Delicate, musky scent. Reproduces from seed, 65–95 per cent successful. Similar to Fragrant Orchid, distinguished by 2 upright ridges on the lip either side of the mouth of the spur, and its pair of pollinia (modified stamens) being removed together, not singly. One of the last downland orchids to flower. No record of pharmaceutical use, but probably used as an aphrodisiac.

RAGGED-ROBIN

THUNDER FLOWER, BACHELORS' BUTTONS

Height 30–76 cm/12–30 in ❀ May–August

Lychnis flos-cuculi
Gk *lukhnos*, lamp; L *flos-cuculi*, cuckoo flower,
flowering in the season of the cuckoo song

An upright perennial of wet meadows. Has
short hairy non-flowering stems and taller
flowering stems. Stalked hairy leaves are
spoon-shaped at base, and opposite, narrow,
lance-shaped above. Distinctive pink (or
white) flowers have 5 deeply cut petals each
divided into 4 narrow lobes, giving a ragged
appearance. Copita-shaped capsule bears
brown seeds. Gerard wrote: 'Not used in
medicine or nourishment, but they serve for
garlands and crowns, and to deck up gardens.'
Old belief that picking the flowers incurred a
thunderstorm, and bunches hung in byres
brought lightning.

RESTHARROW, COMMON

CAMMOCKY, WILD LIQUORICE

Height 20–60 cm/8–24 in ❀ July–September

Ononis repens
Ononis, Gk name used by Pliny for Restharrow
from Gk *onos*, donkey (plant purported to be
their favourite food); L *repens*, creeping
Restharrow, arrests the progress of the harrow

A perennial woody sub-shrub with trailing
stems rooting at intervals. Small toothed oval
or trefoil leaves have tiny leaf-like stipules at
the base clasping the stems. Pink pea-flowers
are borne up erect stems. Seeds are in ovoid
pods. Dry grassland, especially on lime. Spiny
Restharrow (*Ononis spinosa*) is similar, but
always more or less erect and sharply spiny;
the two species hybridise. Mildly diuretic,
purgative. Dried roots used as an infusion for
dropsy, kidney and bladder inflammation, skin
disorders and rheumatism. Children once
chewed the roots like liquorice. Cattle feeding
off it produce 'cammocky', tainted milk.

VALERIAN, COMMON

Height 15–80 cm/6–32 in ❀ June–August

Valeriana officinalis
L *valere*, to be healthy; L *officinalis*, used by
apothecaries for medicinal purposes

A tall, variable perennial with a short conical
rhizome. Single erect stems are hairy near
base. Lower leaves pinnate with a terminal
leaflet; upper leaves unstalked, lance-shaped
irregularly toothed leaflets. Small pinkish-
white flowers in terminal umbrellas.
Individual flowers funnel-shaped, 5-lobed with
3 stamens. Woods, damp and dry grasslands.
Roots have a sedating property; extract used
in many proprietary medicines and herbal
tranquillisers. A maceration of dried roots
used for headaches, nervous heart disorders
and insomnia. Valerian Tea common in
Germany to calm and prevent hysteria.
No side effects but can become addictive.
Cultivated in Derbyshire for medicinal use.

WILLOWHERB, GREAT

CODLINS AND CREAM, GREAT HAIRY
WILLOWHERB, CHERRY PIE

Height 80–150 cm/32–60 in ❀ July–September

Epilobium hirsutum
Gk *epi*, upon; Gk *lobos*, pod; L *hirsutum*, hairy

A hairy perennial, the biggest and largest-
flowered Willowherb. Erect hairy stems bear
opposite stalkless hairy lance-shaped toothed
leaves, half clasping the stems. Stalked flowers
of 4 notched purplish-pink petals are held in a
leafy spike. Seeds in a long slender capsule.
Common in damp areas near water. Of limited
medicinal value but made into tea in Russia.
Named because the leaves resemble those of
the Willow. The name Codlins and Cream
comes from red cooking apples (codlins), after
the colour of the flowers.

WILLOWHERB, ROSEBAY

FIREWEED, BLOOMING SALLY

Height 60–150 cm/24–60 in ✤ June–September

Chamerion angustifolium
Gk *chamae*, on the ground, lowly; Gk *nerion*,
oleander or rosebay; L *angustifolium*, narrow-
leaved; Sally from L *salix*, willow

A sturdy, hairless perennial rising from thick,
spreading, woody roots. Erect, unbranched
stems bear spirally alternate, narrow lance-like
leaves with wavy, slightly toothed edges like
willow. Pink-purple flowers with 4 slightly
notched petals and 4 dark purple sepals borne
in long tapering spikes. A long, slim, 4-sided
capsule below each flower splits when ripe
to release plumed seeds. Spreads aggressively.
Used for stomach complaints and skin
problems. Linnaeus said leaves and young
shoots could be used as vegetables. In Britain
made into an astringent tea; in Russia, used for
Kaporie Tea and, with Fly Agaric fungus, a
potent drink.

BALSAM, ORANGE

JEWEL WEED, SPOTTED TOUCH-ME-NOT

Height up to 150 cm/60 in ❀ July–September

Impatiens capensis
L *impatiens*, impatient (touch-sensitive)
L *capensis*, from the Cape (S. Africa)

A tall delicate branching annual. Alternate
oval to lance-shaped leaves have coarsely
toothed edges. Orange slipper-shaped flowers,
spotted blood red, and with a long slender
crook-shaped spur nestle in the leaf axils.
When ripe, the seed head 'explodes' to scatter
its tiny seeds. Grows along river and canal
banks. Brought here from North America.
The plant has been used in homeopathy as an
emetic, cathartic and diuretic, but is no longer
in use as it is considered to be of questionable
value and safety.

BURNET, SALAD

OLD MAN'S PEPPER, SOT HERB

Height 10–30 cm/4–12 in ❀ May–August

Sanguisorba minor
L *sanguis*, blood; L *sorbeo* from *sorbere*,
to absorb (stops bleeding)
Burnet from Fr *burnete*, brunette

A short greyish tufted perennial. Leaves
mostly at base have 3–12 pairs of deeply
toothed roundish leaflets. Flowers are in dense
globular heads, red-styled female flowers on
top, yellow-stamened male flowers below with
green sepals and no petals. Smells of cucumber
when crushed. Herbal uses against diarrhoea,
wounds, internal bleeding. Fresh juice used for
tuberculosis. Once used as a spice for beer or
brandy. An infusion of leaves is believed to
cure a drunkard's thirst. Young leaves and
shoots used in salads or as vegetables.

PIMPERNEL, SCARLET
POOR MAN'S WEATHERGLASS,
SHEPHERD'S SUNDIAL

Height 5–30 cm/2–12 in ❀ May–October

Anagallis arvensis
Gk *anagallis*, laughing, amusing, delightful
L *arvensis*, of cultivated fields

A prostrate annual with square stems bearing
opposite unstalked pointed-oval shiny leaves
with black glands on undersides. Solitary 5-
petalled red flowers rise from leaf joints on
slender stems. Seeds develop in a globular
capsule. Flowers contain no nectar or scent
and only open for a short time each day,
remaining closed when dull or wet; they are
seldom visited by insects. Ancient Greeks
thought it eased melancholy. Once used
for gallstones, urinary infections, epilepsy,
rheumatism, mental problems, toothache
and snakebite. Used in homeopathy for
skin eruptions, warts, liver and gallbladder
disorders. Leaves can cause dermatitis.

VETCHLING, GRASS
CRIMSON SHOE

Height 10–90 cm/4–36 in ❀ May–July

Lathyrus nissolia
Gk *lathyros*, pea; L *nissolia*, after French
botanist Guillaume Nissole (1647–1735)

A hairless annual, germinating in August,
with long narrow pointed grass-like leaves
(modified stalks). Crimson-red to blue pea-
flowers borne singly or in pairs on long slim
angled stalks. No tendrils. Pale brown hairless
pods hold seeds. Grows in grassy places, in
wayside verges and scrubland. Hard to locate
because it is so grass-like, only the flowers
making it visible.

ALKANET, GREEN

EVERGREEN ALKANET

Height 30–l00 cm/12–40 in ❀ March–July

Pentaglottis sempervirens
Gk *penta*, five; Gk *glottis*, tongue
L *sempervirens*, evergreen
Alkanet from Arabic *al-hinna*, henna, a shrub
with roots yielding a red dye

A tufted bristly perennial with an upright
branched stem bearing hairy stalked oval
leaves. Upper leaves unstalked and paler
below. Flat white-eyed blue flowers with
5 petals borne in long coils that uncurl as the
flowers mature. Seeds are 4 nutlets with raised
edges. Medicinal use similar to Comfrey (both
are in the Borage family). It is commonly
found near habitations, where it was formerly
cultivated for medicinal uses. Used formerly
by monks as a red dye.

BELLFLOWER, CLUSTERED

FOOL'S GENTIAN

Height 5–30 cm/2–12 in ❀ June–October

Campanula glomerata
L *campanula*, little bell
L *glomerata*, gathered together

A roughly hairy perennial with erect,
sometimes angled, reddish stems and long-
stalked, heart-shaped, toothed leaves
clutching the stem. Upper leaves narrower.
Deep violet-blue, erect gentian-like trumpet-
shaped flowers are clustered in a dense head.
Occasionally a pale violet or white flower
occurs. A plant of grassland, open woods and
waste places on chalk or limestone, often
confused in bud with the Autumn Gentian.

BELLFLOWER, NETTLE-LEAVED

NETTLE-LEAVED BLUEBELL, BATS IN
THE BELFRY, THROAT-WORT

Height 60–100 cm/24–40 in ✿ June–September

Campanula trachelium
L *campanula*, little bell; L *trachelus* from Gk
trachelos, neck (used for throat infections)

Erect, roughly hairy, angled stems bear pointed
ovate coarsely toothed short-stalked nettle-
like leaves. Violet or blue 5-petalled ascending
flowers with a leaf-like raceme are often in
small clusters. The top flowers open first. Seed
capsules droop. Grows in woodland or scrub
over limestone and chalk, particularly in S.
England. Early botanists called this plant
Canterbury Bell because of its abundance in
woods near that city, but it is unrelated to
the garden species. Alternative name Throat-
wort reveals former medicinal usage. The
chopped roots were used as a gargle for
tonsillitis and sore throats. Young shoots
can be cooked as a vegetable.

BLUEBELL

HYACINTH, SQUILL, CROWTOES

Height 20–50 cm/8–20 in ✿ April–June

Hyacinthoides non-scripta
Gk *hyacinthoides*, hyacinth-like
L *non-scripta*, not written about (to distinguish
it from the Hyacinth written about in Gk
mythology)

White bulb gives rise to narrowish strap-like
leaves. Flowers on a drooping one-sided spike,
blue, bell-shaped, honey scented. Fruit capsule
splits into 8 segments to disperse black seeds.
Bulbs do not multiply. Plants can be destroyed
by trampling. Bulbs contain starch used in
Elizabethan times to stiffen ruffs and cuffs.
Also used to make glue. Considered unlucky
to bring into dwellings.

BORAGE

Height 15–70 cm/6–28 in ❀ **May–September**

Borago officinalis
Medieval L *borrago* from Arabic *abu huras*,
father of roughness (denoting leaf surface)
L *officinalis*, used by apothecaries for medicinal
purposes

A stout erect hairy annual with stalked lower
ovate to lance-shaped wavy-edged leaves,
unstalked upper. Large bright blue flowers
with 5 pointed petals, a white centre and a
cone of black stamens, hang in bunches. Seeds
4 dark nutlets. Waysides, rough and waste
ground. According to Pliny it 'maketh a man
merry and joyfull'. Medicinally it is a diuretic,
demulcent and emollient, most useful for
fevers, lung and kidney disorders. Young
shoots once used in salads or boiled as a
vegetable, having a cucumber-like fragrance,
that also makes a cooling drink.

BROOKLIME

LIMEWORT

Height 20–60 cm/8–24 in ❀ **May–September**

Veronica beccabunga
After St Veronica who accompanied Christ
to the cross (for another derivation, see
Speedwell, Germander); ON *bekkr*, beck;
ON *bung*, block; Brooklime from OE *brok*,
brook; L *limus*, lime (plaster)

A hairless sprawling fleshy perennial of small
streams and wet places. Hollow creeping often
rooting stems give rise to erect sometimes
reddish flowering stems with opposite short-
stalked bluntly toothed fleshy leaves. Bright
blue white-eyed, four unequal-petalled flowers
rise from leaf joints, in opposite slim-stalked
spikes of up to 30. Fruits are in rounded
capsules. Leaves edible (though not very
palatable) in salads but once used for scurvy.
Used in some diet drinks, and as a blood
purge. In medieval times used for gout and
other swellings.

BUGLE

THUNDER AND LIGHTNING

Height 8–30 cm/3–12 in ❦ **April–July**

Ajuga reptans
Possibly a corruption of L *abigo*, I drive away
(disease); L *reptans*, creeping

A woodland perennial with creeping, rooting
runners. Has a rosette of long-stalked ovate
leaves, purple beneath. Unstemmed stalk
leaves opposite, often purplish, up a stiff stem.
Pale blue flowers in whorls above stem leaves.
Short upper lip exposes blue stamens. Fruit is a
short bell-shaped tube containing 4 nutlets.
Medieval herbalists grew it widely as a cure-
all. Culpeper advised a syrup of Bugle for
'wounds, thrusts and stabs, ulcers and broken
bones'. Recommended for delirium tremens.
Still in use, infusion of Bugle and Peppermint
taken for dyspepsia and gallbladder disorders.

CHICORY

WILD SUCCORY

Height 30–120 cm/12–48 in ❦ **June–September**

Cichorium intybus
Gk *kikhorion*, endive; L *intybus* from Egyptian
tybi, January (the month when it was eaten)

An erect perennial rising from a Dandelion-
like tap root. Hairy basal leaves also like
Dandelion have deeply divided and more
pointed lobes. Many-branched grooved stems
bear stalkless upper leaves and clusters of
striking blue flowers in twos or threes with
rayed and toothed blunt-ended florets.
Normally, only a few flowers are in bloom at
one time, opening with the sun and closing
about midday. Seeds are tiny ovoid nutlets.
A diuretic, used for dyspepsia. Country folk
believed that water distilled from the flowers
was good for the sight and against eye
inflammation. Cultivated both for salad use
and as animal fodder. Dried roasted roots
make a bitter drink alone or added to coffee.

HAREBELL

SCOTTISH BLUEBELL, WITCHES' THIMBLES,
FAIRY BELLS, DEVIL'S BELL, WITCH BELL

Height 15–40 cm/6–16 in   ❋ July–October

Campanula rotundifolia
L *campanula*, little bell
L *rotundifolia*, round-leaved

A perennial with a creeping underground
stolon producing unbranched slender erect
stems. Basal leaves round or heart-shaped on
short stalks. Upper leaves unstalked, lance-
shaped. Hanging blue flowers bell-shaped.
Fruit capsule releases a few seeds at a time
from basal pores. The round leaves at the base
wither before the flowers come out. Whereas
the English Bluebell is a Hyacinth, in parts
of Scotland, as in the song, these are the
'blue bells of Scotland'. The common names
relating to witches are linked to the hare's
role as a witch animal in folk myth.

MILKWORT, COMMON

ROGATION FLOWER

Height 5–10 cm/2–4 in   ❋ May–September

Polygala vulgaris
Gk *poly*, much; Gk *gala*, milk
L *vulgaris*, common

A perennial with a woody rootstock. No
rosette but upright slender stems bear
alternate oval to elliptic leaves. The flowers
have 3 tiny green sepals and 2 big bluish inner
sepals cradling the tube of 5 petals fused
together. The lowest petal is fringed. Flowers
can be blue, white or pink. Flowers considered
to resemble udders, therefore infusions
believed to increase mothers' milk. Valuable
in herbal medicines for respiratory problems,
as an expectorant and cough cure. It was
carried in Rogation Week ceremonies on
20 May. Chalk Milkwort (*Polygala calcarea*)
occurs at Hartslock BBOWT Reserve (Walk
3), and is recognisable by its irregular false
rosette of blunter leaves at the stem base.

SPEEDWELL, COMMON FIELD

Height up to 50 cm/20 in ❀ Year-long

Veronica persica
L *veronica*, after St Veronica who
accompanied Christ to the cross, or
Gk *phero*, I bring, and Gk *nike*, victory
L *persica*, from Persia

A sprawling, hairy annual with short-stalked,
oval, coarsely toothed, grey-green leaves.
Bright blue solitary 4-petalled flowers are
carried on slim stalks in the axils of the upper
leaves. The lower petal is often very pale or
white. Seed capsules with prominent ridges
are borne on recurved stalks. A native of Iran
and other parts of Western Asia, naturalised
all over UK on cultivated or disturbed ground,
presumably to improve grazing. The astringent
bitter diuretic leaves were in use by herbalists
from an early date.

SPEEDWELL, GERMANDER

BONNY BIRD'S EYE, BREAK-YOUR-
MOTHER'S-HEART

Height 10–30 cm/4–12 in ❀ April–July

Veronica chamaedrys
L *veronica*, after St Veronica who
accompanied Christ to the cross, or
Gk *phero*, I bring, and Gk *nike*, victory
Gk *chamaedrys*, dwarf oak (referring to lobed,
oak-like leaves); Germander possibly a
corruption of Gk *chamaedrys*

A slim hairy perennial with hairs in 2 opposite
lines down stems, often prostrate at base.
Leaves dark green coarsely toothed. Brilliant
sky-blue flowers with white centres borne in
stalked bunches at base of leaves. Hairy heart-
shaped capsule cradles seeds. Astringent, once
used to purify the blood. In Ireland, boiled
in milk for jaundice. In Guernsey, as a tea
for indigestion and stomach pains. Little
medicinal value. The common name
Speedwell implies that it is quick to heal.

SPEEDWELL, IVY-LEAVED

Height up to 60 cm/24 in ✤ **February–August**

Veronica hederifolia
L *veronica*, after St Veronica who
accompanied Christ to the cross, or
Gk *phero*, I bring, and Gk *nike*, victory
L *hederifolia*, ivy-leaved

A sprawling, hairy annual with branching
stems bearing kidney-shaped, opposite, 5–7-
lobed leaves on short stalks. Small pale lilac
or blue 4-petalled flowers grow on very short
stalks in leaf axils. Seeds in a hairless round
capsule. The English name Speedwell can also
mean goodbye, referring to the rapid petal-
drop if the flowers are picked.

SPEEDWELL, THYME-LEAVED

THYME SPEEDWELL

Height 5–25 cm/2–10 in ✤ **April–October**

Veronica serpyllifolia
L *veronica*, after St Veronica who
accompanied Christ to the cross, or
Gk *phero*, I bring, and Gk *nike*, victory
L *serpens*, creeping; L *folia*, leaves

A slightly downy creeping perennial, rooting
frequently. Shiny short-stalked untoothed oval
leaves grow in opposite pairs. Pale blue 4-
petalled flowers borne in leafy terminal spikes.
Seed capsule heart-shaped and hairy. Culpeper
says: 'Venus governs this plant, and it is
among the vulnerary plants, used both
inwardly and outwardly; it is also pectoral and
good for coughs and consumptions; the stone
and the strangury, and against pestilential
fevers'. Speedwell implies it is quick to heal,
or it may come from the good-luck buttonhole
given in Ireland to those about to set off on
a journey.

SPEEDWELL, WOOD

Height up to 50 cm/20 in   🌸 April–July

Veronica montana
L *veronica*, after St Veronica who
accompanied Christ to the cross, or
Gk *phero*, I bring, and Gk *nike*, victory
L *montana*, of the mountains

A sprawling perennial with hairy stems and
long-stalked, oval, coarsely toothed leaves
held in opposite pairs. Long stalks bear pale
lilac-blue, 4-petalled flowers. Kidney-shaped
capsules hold seeds. Common in damp and
clay woodland. In England it is also an
indicator of ancient woodland.

VIPER'S-BUGLOSS

Height 30–60 cm/12–24 in   🌸 June–September

Echium vulgare
Gk *ekhis*, she-viper; L *vulgare*, common

An upright bristly biennial of light dry soils,
often on lime. Speckled hairy stems have basal
leaves like an ox tongue covered with white
hairs and a prominent midriff. Flowers are
borne in coiled sprays forming a prominent
snake's-head-like spike. Flower buds are pink,
bright blue when open, the sprays gradually
uncoiling. Close up, the flowers resemble
gentians. Long pointed sepals nurture 4
angular nutlets. Sweat-inducing and diuretic,
used since ancient Greek times to ease
lumbago; increase mothers' milk; for coughs
and chest conditions, and for skin complaints.
The seeds resembling snake heads were
thought to cure snakebites. Once believed
effective against sadness and melancholy.
Toxic alkaloids debar internal use.

HELLEBORINE, VIOLET

CLUSTERED HELLEBORINE

Height up to 60 cm/24 in   ❀ late July–August

Epipactis purpurata
Epipactis, ancient Gk name used by
Theophrastus for milk-curdling plant
L *purpurata*, purplish

Deep-rooted much-divided descending
rootstock produces a single flowering stem at
first then, as it matures, clusters of stems. Each
stem bears 5–10 narrow purplish-grey leaves,
spirally arranged, and a flower-spike bearing
many closely spaced greenish flowers with
pointed sepals and petals and a pale green lip
to a basal cup that has a purplish inside. This
plant grows best in beechwoods, often in deep
shade, where few other plants can survive.
A plant of ancient southern woodlands.

LORDS-AND-LADIES

CUCKOO PINT, ADAM AND EVE, SWEETHEARTS, WILD ARUM

Height 30–45 cm/12–18 in   ❀ April–June

Arum maculatum
Arum, name given by Theophrastus
L *maculatum*, spotted (the spathe)

A fleshy perennial tuber gives rise to stalked
arrow-shaped leaves, often spotted purple or
brown. An upright stem bears a purplish-green
cylindrical flower head surrounded by a pale
green spathe or hood, sometimes spotted.
Pollinated by insects crawling through down-
pointing hairs. Fruits on a spike initially green,
turn into orange-red fleshy berries that are
VERY POISONOUS. English names have
sexual connotations. Starchy roots made into
Portland sago or arrowroot for gruel, and as
starch for hair and beards and stiffening
clothes (mixing by hand caused blisters).
Tubers also used as soap. Mixed with rose
water to whiten face.

MERCURY, DOG'S

SNAKEWEED

Height: up to 40 cm/16 in ❀ February–May

Mercurialis perennis
Named after Mercury, its alleged discoverer
L *perennis*, perennial

A creeping perennial with upright
unbranched 4-sided stems, with pairs of
toothed hairy leaves. Insignificant petal-less
greenish flowers are female. Male flowers
have identical sepals and petals in whorls of 3.
Male and female on separate plants. Hairy
seed has 3 rounded segments. Annual Mercury
once used as a purgative and diuretic. The
poisonous leaves must never be eaten. Called
'Dog's' because herbalists considered it unfit
for human use. Once called Bad Henry,
as opposed to the edible and virtuous Good
King Henry.

MOSCHATEL

TOWN HALL CLOCK, MUSKWEED,
MUSK RANUNCULUS

Height 10–15 cm/4–6 in ❀ March–May

Adoxa moschatellina
Gk *adoxa*, without glory (its small greenish
flowers often go unnoticed)
L *moschata*, musky smell

A low, slender hairless perennial with long-
stalked leaves divided into three lobed leaflets,
rather like a Wood Anemone. Five-faceted
green flowers held erect on slender stems with
one flower on each of 4 sides and one facing
upwards. Green fruits like tiny acorns. When
damp or at dusk it smells of musk. The scent
has also been likened to almond and elder
blossom. On hedge banks at lower levels, but
shy and hard to spot, though can be locally
profuse. The only species in its family, it is
such a strange plant that in the past botanists
were unsure how to classify it and some placed
it with the buttercups.

ORCHID, FROG

Height 5–25 cm/2–10 in ❀ June–August

Coeloglossum viride
Gk *koilos*, hollow; Gk *glossa*, tongue
(together signifying the lip of the flower)
L *viridis*, fresh green

A short, inconspicuous orchid somewhat like
a Twayblade. At the base of the plant are
2 forked tubers, one for the current year's
blossoming, the other preparing for the next.
2–5 broad, blunt leaves swathe the lower stem,
few upper leaves thinner and shorter. Short
flower spike bears, between bracts, a number
of flowers supposedly like a jumping frog,
yellowish-green tinged with reddish-brown.
The globular helmet sits over a longer strap-
like lip with 3 short teeth at the end, and a
short spur. Grows in short grassland on lime
in S. England; elsewhere in meadows and on
mountain ledges and dunes.

PLANTAIN, HOARY

Height 7.5–30 cm/3–12 in ❀ May–August

Plantago media
L *planta*, sole of foot (how some leaves hug the
ground); L *media*, middle-sized

A greyish perennial of lime-rich soils. All the
leaves forming a basal rosette are broad oval
narrowing to a winged stalk with prominent
ribs and covered with white hairs. Erect hairy
stalks bear a dense cylindrical spike of grey-
green flowers with prominent pale pink-purple
stamens. The only plantain with a delicate
perfume that attracts insects. Its seeds are very
popular with small birds. Grassland, usually
limy. Gerard wrote: 'The juice dropped in the
eyes cools the heat and inflammation thereof.
The seeds boiled in milk are laxative and
demulcent. The leaves rubbed into the
stems of fruit trees afflicted with blight
effect a ready cure.'

SPURGE, WOOD

DEVIL'S CUP AND SAUCER

Height up to 90 cm/36 in ❀ March–May

Euphorbia amygdaloides
L *euphorbia*, from Euphorbus, physician to
King Juba of Mauritania who used the plant
medicinally; Gk *amygdaloides*, almond-like

An evergreen perennial with erect
unbranched stems that bear narrow lance-
shaped leaves, often tinged red and crowded
at the top. The flowers lack petals and sepals,
consisting of oval yellowy-green bracts fused
into a saucer-shaped collar. Greenish-yellow
capsules holding blackish seeds are borne on
short stalks within the 'saucer'. The common
spring Spurge of southern woodlands; Sun and
Petty Spurges are fairly common later in the
year in the Chilterns. The root bark was once
used to treat fevers, but not considered very
safe – in Africa, plants of the same family
were used to provide poison for arrow tips!

TWAYBLADE, COMMON

SWEETHEARTS, SWAYBLADE

Height 30–60 cm/12–24 in ❀ May–July

Listera ovata
Named after English physician and naturalist
Martin Lister (1638–1712); L *ovata*, oval
Tway, archaic form of two (leaves)

An all-green orchid with a short thick creeping
rhizome with a large tuft of sinuous roots. Each
year the rhizome grows up to a flowering stem,
and growth continues underground from a
lateral bud. A single pair of opposite unstalked
oval leaves appears. Long stem bears flower
spike of yellow-green flowers with a long
narrow lip, forked and unspurred. Pollinated by
small insects. Germinating seeds need 4 years
of mycorhizal support, then 10 more years
before flowering; the plant depends more on
vegetative multiplication. Often flowers in
groups, in woods and grassy places. Probably
Britain's most common and widely distributed
orchid. Gerard used it in ointment.

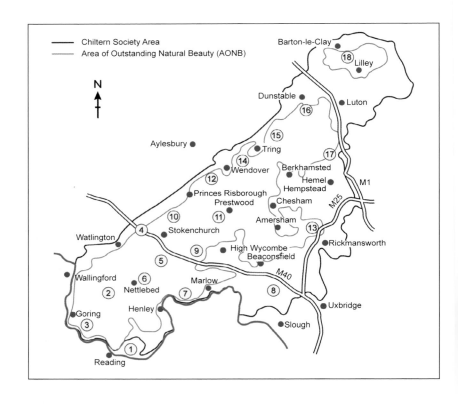

SYMBOLS USED IN THE MAPS

═══	Road	🍄	Wood
·········	Track or bridleway	☁	Scrub
───	River or canal	▲	Hilltop
─ ─ ─	Walking route	＼｜／	Viewpoint
·········	Alternative walking route	■	Building
++++++	Railway	✝	Church or chapel
▼▼▼	Upper Slopes Lower	Ⓟ	Parking
		ⓦⓒ	Toilets

WALKS

		km	miles	hours
1	SONNING EYE	8.5	5¼	2¾–3¾
2	NUFFIELD	9.25	5¾	3½–4½
3	GORING	8.75	5½	2¾–3¾
4	ASTON ROWANT	7.25	4½	2¾–4
5	TURVILLE HEATH	14.75	9¼	5¼–6½
6	WARBURG	12	7½	3¾–5
7	HAMBLEDEN	10.75	6¾	3½–4½
8	FULMER	7.25	4½	2–3
9	WEST WYCOMBE	14.5	9	4½–6
10	CHINNOR HILL	12	7½	3½–4½
11	PRESTWOOD	8.5	5¼	3–4
12	PULPIT HILL	10	6¼	3½–4½
13	CHENIES	8.75	5½	2½–3½
14	WENDOVER	10	6¼	3½–4½
15	PITSTONE HILL	13.5	8½	4½–5½
16	DUNSTABLE DOWNS	7.25	4½	2¼–3½
17	GADDESDEN	6	3¾	2–3
18A	PEGSDON	6.5	4	2–3
18B	BARTON HILLS	2.5	1½	1–2

INTRODUCTION TO THE WALKS

The walks have been carefully selected to pass through some of the most interesting botanical areas, as well as including places of geographical and historical interest. In addition, the routes offer picturesque landscapes – often from an elevated viewpoint – making them classic walks in their own right. In some cases the walks will reveal carpets of prolific colonies, and in others the opportunity to see often isolated species of very rare flowers. With the aid of the Directory pictures and descriptions, the flowering charts and the list of which species to look out for, discovery and recognition should not be difficult. All the walks are on public or permissive footpaths unless Open Access is mentioned.

The maps have been drawn to show only relevant landmarks and features. Walk routes are indicated by a line of red dashes (with shortcuts indicated by red dots), and by red arrows to indicate preferred direction but since all the walks are circular, they can be taken in the opposite direction.

Most walks would be classified as easy and the times given assume a gentle pace of two miles per hour with adequate stopping time for flower identification and photography. All the walks involve some measure of ascent, but seldom steeply. Each is well within the compass of any reasonably fit person under the age of ninety.

The best footwear is walking boots or strong shoes with grooved soles, although in dry periods trainers would suffice.

Ordnance Survey references are to the Outdoor Leisure Maps. The Chiltern Society maps are targeted at walkers, clearly showing footpaths, bridleways – and the nearest public house!

Most of the reserves visited belong to the Berkshire, Buckinghamshire and Oxfordshire Wildlife Trust (BBOWT) or English Nature (EN), although one or two are run by local councils. Many have informative notice boards at their boundaries.

ABBREVIATIONS USED IN WALK DESCRIPTIONS

L	left
R	right
(R)	Reserve
KG	kissing gate
PH	public house
BW	bridleway
CP	car park
FP	footpath
FB	footbridge
NT	National Trust

Opposite: autumn colours in beech wood (Walk 12).

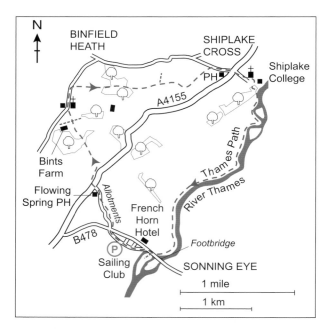

Map: use OS Explorer 171, Chiltern Society Map 4

Teasels by the
River Thames.

WALK 1 ◆ SONNING EYE

Distance 8.5 km / 5¼ miles
Time 2¾–3¾ hours

Park along dead-end side road just past boathouse entrance off B478 at Sonning Eye (SU 751759).

Walk NW to end of lane, cross B478 and enter allotments through KG. Skirt along hedge, back on to Spring Lane, and continue to Flowing Spring PH. Cross A4155 on to permissive path, turning R along field edge, passing through gap in hedge, then L up yellow arrowed path by fence, and L again up hill. Ignore turning L to Bint's Farm and continue as far as road, turning R to pass chapel. After 360 m along road, follow FP R signed to Shiplake, along field edge and through wood. Follow yellow arrows L around next field, through hedge at telegraph poles and straight on, R then L to Shiplake Cross. Turn R then cross A4155 and walk down Church Lane, past church, through field gate and then follow blue arrowed BW R, descending in zigzag towards river. Go L then R to pass around boathouse, and immediately over footbridge. Follow Thames Path back to Sonning. Turn R on B478, taking FP L opposite French Horn Hotel, between Furleigh Cottages and public car park. Continue back to start. NB: Path is close to deep water in places.

LOOK OUT FOR

March	Common Field and Ivy-leaved Speedwells, Red Dead-nettle
April	Cuckooflower, Garlic Mustard, Summer Snowflake
May	Common Comfrey, Common Vetch, Hedgerow Crane's-bill
June	Bladder Campion, Field Pansy, Hemlock Water-dropwort
July	Black Horehound, Marsh Woundwort, Tufted Vetch
August	Sneezewort, Purple-loosestrife, Wild Angelica
September	Hemp-agrimony, Himalayan Balsam, Perennial Sow-thistle

Birds and butterflies to note may include Buzzard, Red Kite, Swan; Green Hairstreak, Ringlet, Small Heath

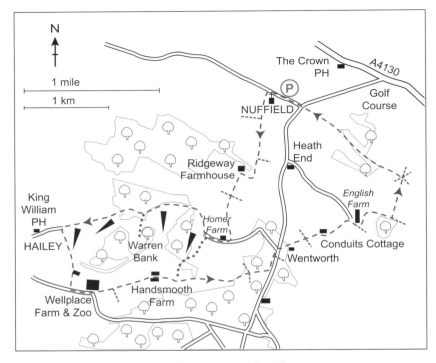

Map: use OS Explorer 171, Chiltern Society Map 15

WALK 2 • NUFFIELD

Distance 9.25 km / 5³/₄ miles
Time 3¹/₂–4¹/₂ hours

Park along Nuffield Hill, opposite Old
School (SU 669873).

Walk along road past church, then L
signed Ridgeway. When Ridgeway turns
R in woods, continue straight ahead,
round Ridgeway Farm house, and down
between Homer House and barn to track,
where turn R [shortcut after c. 250 m,
turn L just after Homer Cottage and
rejoin route L] following wide track
towards Hailey. [To visit Warren Bank
BBOWT Reserve: at bend in clearing
c. 800 m past Homer Cottage, follow
track L, through field gate and straight
across field, entering reserve through KG
by information board.] Take FP L signed
Chiltern Way Extension down hill, then
L at road past Wellplace Zoo. At bend in
road, continue straight ahead up track
signed Urquhart Lane. Continue up hill
and through wood to main road where
turn L for c. 450 m then R on FP
opposite entrance to Homer Farm Drive.
Follow arrows through wood then round
cottage, cross lane and over next field
to pass R between Conduits Cottage and
tennis court. Go L at drive then over
cattle grid and down to English Farm,
where go R round central barn, then L
downhill and up other side. Turn L at
gate and follow hedge to junction of six
paths. Turn L then L again to go through
wood back to Nuffield. At Elderberry
Cottage, go L along FP to return to start.

Opposite: Handsmooth near Hailey.

LOOK OUT FOR

March	Lesser Celandine, Snowdrop, White Dead-nettle
April	Dog and Sweet Violets, Moschatel, Wood Anemone
May	Dove's-foot Crane's-bill, Germander Speedwell, Wood Avens
June	Bee Orchid (R), Hedge Woundwort, Wild Mignonette
July	Dwarf Thistle, Fool's Parsley, Yellow-wort
August	Common Field Speedwell, Red Bartsia, Nettle-leaved Bellflower
September	Herb-Robert, Devil's-bit Scabious, Yarrow

Birds and butterflies to note may
include Pheasant, Red Kite,
Woodpeckers; Dark Green
Fritillary, Small Heath, Marbled
White

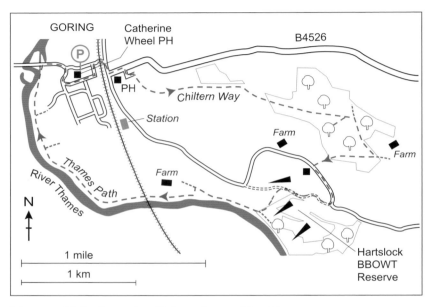

Map: use OS Explorer 171, Chiltern Society Map 16

WALK 3 ◆ GORING

Distance 8.75 km / 5½ miles
Time 2¾–3¾ hours

Park in public CP behind Catherine Wheel PH, Station Road, Goring (SU 601806).

Exit L along Station Road, turn L at end along Red Cross Road then R across railway bridge. Go R again to follow B4526 round past pub, and then second R into Whitehills Green. At end of cul de sac, go through narrow path and KG, following arrow direction along Chiltern Way, diagonally L across playing field, then skirting hedge to L round next field. Enter wood at bottom of dip, still following Chiltern Way and ignoring forest tracks. Take R turn at next two T-junctions, eventually leaving wood by barns. Follow direction of arrow L along surfaced track and at middle of S-bend, go straight ahead then R down sunken path. At bottom of hill, turn L into reserve outskirts. Take L gate to enter and explore inner reserve area, keeping to permissive path as shown on information board. Exit inner reserve and continue round grassy bank, down through wood, turning R at riverside track. Follow finger post 'Thames Path' L through paddocks, then follow riverbank R all the way to Goring, back up to main road and R round Manor Road/Station Road to CP. NB: River path close to deep water in places.

LOOK OUT FOR

March	Dog Violets, Colt's-foot, Dog's Mercury
April	Bluebell, Ground-ivy, Summer Snowflake
May	Common Comfrey, Cut-leaved Crane's-bill, White Campion, Lady & Monkey Orchids (R)
June	Field Madder, Hedge Bedstraw, Hemlock
July	Enchanter's-nightshade, Greater Knapweed, Wild Parsnip
August	Common Fleabane, Purple-loosestrife, Autumn Gentian (R)
September	Orange Balsam, Common & Pale Toadflax, Clustered Bellflower (R)

Birds and butterflies to note may include Heron, Cormorant, Long-tailed Tit, Red Kite; Chalkhill Blue, Green Hairstreak, Adonis Blue

Opposite: Teasel and Hogweed seed heads.

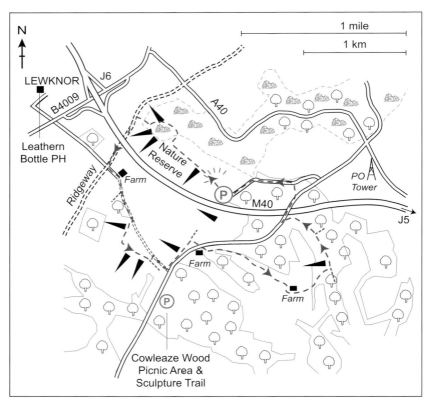

Map: use OS Explorer 171, Chiltern Society Map 9

WALK 4 ◆ ASTON ROWANT

Distance 7.25 km / 4½ miles
Time 2¾–4 hours

Park at Aston Rowant English Nature
Reserve CP (SU 731966), signposted
from Christmas Common road (off A40).

Leave CP by right-hand information
board to viewpoint. Continue along
contour (follow brown arrow) to end of
ridge. At second brown arrow, continue
as signed to plastic post with green arrow,
where turn L down hill through metal
field gate, then R following fence line
steeply down to bottom track. Go R
then L, leaving the Reserve and joining
Ridgeway. Turn L under the M40, then
L again up surfaced lane. At farmhouse,
fork R, continuing up wide track to
second arrow post, where turn R by
information board and go diagonally L up
hill, through metal gate and along hedge
to arrow post. Go L across field, then R
up track and L along BW parallel with
road. 20 m beyond disused road surface,
turn R along fence line to road, crossing
to enter Wormsley Estate, following drive
down and past Lower Vicars Farm. Turn
L through garden gate, following yellow
arrow round yew hedge and diagonally up
into wood. Follow white arrows on trees.
Near top of hill, go L along track and
back on to road. Turn R, crossing M40
cutting and, after 200 m, go L at FP sign
up steps and through larch copse, then L
on road back to CP.
NB: The Reserve area is Open Access so
it is possible to explore off-path.

LOOK OUT FOR

April	Wood Spurge, Yellow Archangel, Dog Violets
May	Cowslip, Common Milkwort (R), Salad Burnet
June	Dropwort, Wild Candytuft (R), Greater Butterfly & Bee Orchids (R)
July	Clustered Bellflower, Frog Orchid (R), Musk Thistle
August	Ploughman's-spikenard, Common Toadflax, Carline Thistle
September	Autumn & Chiltern Gentians (R), Eyebright, Dark Mullein

Birds and butterflies to note may
include Goldfinch, Skylark, Red
Kite; Brown Argus, Silver-spotted
Skipper, Dark Green Fritillary

The Vale of Aylesbury from Aston Rowant
Nature Reserve.

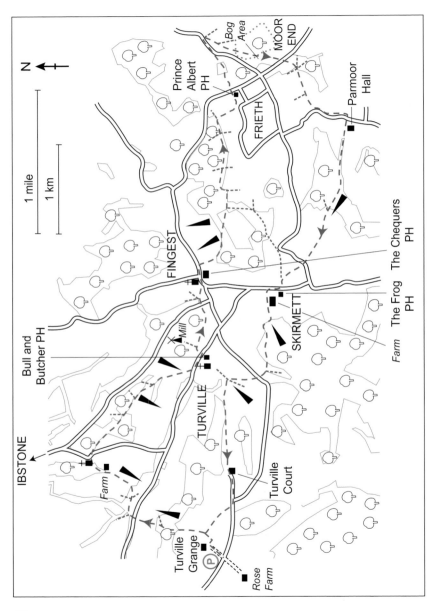

WALK 5 ♦ TURVILLE HEATH

Distance 14.75 km / 9¼ miles
Time 5¼–6½ hours

Park at Turville Heath opposite drive to
Rose Farm (SU 744909).

Walk up drive to Turville Grange where
briefly R then L through field gate and
over stile, L down through wood and
cross valley bottom road. Take BW
forking R, then FP through woods
following arrows. Climb steeply to water
trough, then R through Ibstone
Churchyard. At lane go briefly R then L
along wood edge FP. Proceed through
woods to obvious fork. Go R and drop
down to Turville. Go L opposite phone
box then R on Chiltern Way through
Fingest, R up hill to fork [R fork is short-
cut to Skirmett], where L to T-junction.
Bear L round walled garden to end of
wood, then R to join lane, where L across
field to road, then R.

Just before PH, L on to FP off track,
then R at top of rise, heading for
building. Go R along drive, then L along
main road past bus stop. At bend, fork
back R past cottages and Kings Corner,
along wall then R into woods following
arrows. Pass Apple Cottage, straight on
over FB, then fork R past boggy area to
cross road. Over stile, follow arrows, then
L at track. At junction, go R up side of
fence, cross open field to barn and road,
L past farm, then along roadside FP. At
double bend, fork R past back of
Parmoor Hall. Continue down sunken
path, crossing lane, to Skirmett, where
R. Leave road L up drive past tennis
court. Skirt round wood, following FP
signs, then R down past gas pipes. Cross
lane and field, then L steeply up hill to
pass Turville Court, down drive to join
lane where immediately R across fields
to Turville Grange and CP.

LOOK OUT FOR

April	Primrose, Wood-sorrel, Wood Anemone
May	Bluebell, Woodruff, Ground-ivy
June	Chicory, Lucerne, Southern Marsh Orchid
July	Agrimony, Common Toadflax, Nettle-leaved Bellflower
August	Tormentil, Betony, Sneezewort, Wild Angelica
September	Scarlet Pimpernel, Pale Toadflax, Fluellens

Birds to note may include Red Kite,
Pheasant, Skylark

Map: use OS Explorer 171, Chiltern Society Map 11

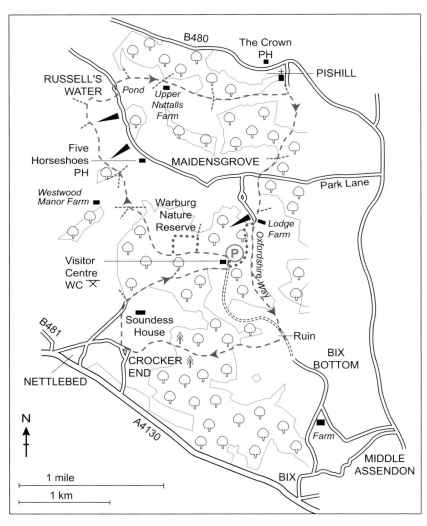

Map: use OS Explorer 171, Chiltern Society Maps 2 and 9

WALK 6 ◆ WARBURG

Distance 12 km / 7½ miles
Time 3¾–5 hours

Park at Warburg BBOWT Reserve CP
(SU 720878).

Leave CP by information shelter; after
10 m, L along mown FP, through KG,
and on to sunken track. [Detour R to see
Gentians.] Turn L, then R on BW out of
Reserve to Westwood Manor Farm track.
Turn R along valley bottom to fork, then
R to reach Russell's Water. At road, turn
L then R round pond, L past Pond
Cottage, R past houses, straight on to L
of dell, across open common to Upper
Nuttalls Farm. Pass between barns and
follow BW along wood edge to Pishill.
Turn R to join Oxfordshire Way,
eventually crossing road then past Lodge
Farm. Turn R then L. [Shortcut: almost
immediately take FP R, then L, steeply
down through Reserve to CP.] Continue
down, forking R through wood,
descending to road at valley bottom.
Turn L then R past ruins and into wood.
As path leaves track, follow arrows on
trees, past yews and into field. Keep
hedge to L, then R through Crocker End
and R again at Chiltern Way signpost.
Cross field, L of 3 cedars, R on to lane
then straight ahead on BW back to
Visitor Centre.
An informative leaflet showing the paths
round the Reserve is available at the
Visitor Centre.
NB: This Reserve is NOT Open Access –
keep to marked paths.

LOOK OUT FOR

March	Lesser Celandine, Wood Anemone, Sweet Violet (White)
April	Greater Stitchwort, Wood-sorrel, Wood Spurge
May	Bugle, Ramsons, Garlic Mustard, Yellow Archangel
June	Pale Toadflax, Pyramidal Orchid, Vervain
July	Common Centaury, Greater Knapweed, St John's-wort
August	Wild Parsnip, Eyebright, Marjoram
September	Scarlet Pimpernel, Autumn & Chiltern Gentians (R), Harebell

Birds and butterflies to note may
include Red Kite, Pheasant,
Warblers, Woodpeckers;
Grizzled Skipper, Purple Emperor,
Purple Hairstreak

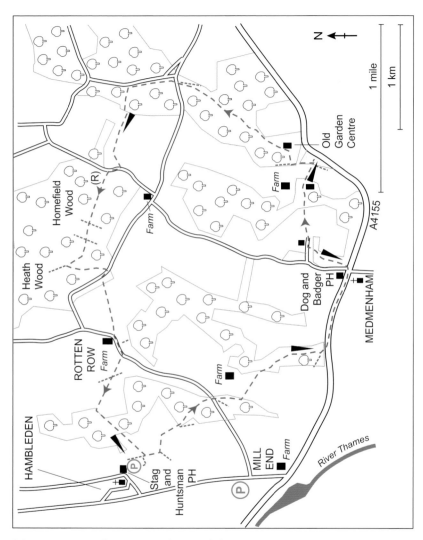

Map: use OS Explorer 171 and 172, Chiltern Society Maps 1 and 11

WALK 7 ◆ HAMBLEDEN

Distance 10.75 km / 6¾ miles
Time 3½–4½ hours

Park in public CP beyond Stag & Huntsman PH (SU 786866).

Leave far end of CP, go L across playing field then R on wide track, forking L up hill where track divides. Follow FP R along hedge into wood and up to cross road. Take FP bearing L, skirting edge of wood. At recently planted area, follow yellow arrow on finger post, then descend to main road, where L for 450 m to Dog & Badger PH. Turn L then immediately R into wood up steep hill. At top, follow white arrows to Old School House, where turn R. At end of lane, skirt L round The Hermitage, dropping to valley bottom. Take FP L, then L again along wood edge. At fingerpost, go R straight up steep hill to drive, then L past old garden centre and L again (signed permissive path) through top of wood, keeping to fence line then following white arrows on trees to road junction. Take FP straight ahead parallel with road to join Chiltern Way, where turn L, following white arrows steeply down hill and over stile at bottom. At next road, go R then L into Homefield Wood along wide forestry track. [Almost immediately R is the BBOWT Reserve.] Continue to bend and fingerpost, turn sharp L, climbing back up to road, then R for 160 m, and L signed Chiltern Way to Rotten Row. Walk down lane then R through fields into woods, down hill and back to Hambleden.

LOOK OUT FOR

March	Dog & Sweet Violets, Primrose, Ground-ivy
April	Wood Anemone, Wood Spurge, Wood-sorrel
May	Wild Strawberry, Yellow Pimpernel, Thyme-leaved Speedwell, Military Orchid (R)
June	Bittersweet, Creeping Cinquefoil, Stinking Iris
July	Wild Catmint, Silverweed, Wild Basil
August	Ploughman's-spikenard, Yarrow, Hemp-agrimony
September	Selfheal, Scentless Mayweed, White Dead-nettle

Birds and butterflies to note may include Red Kite, Chiffchaff, Cuckoo; Silverwashed Fritillary, Marbled White, Common Blue

View of Hambleden.

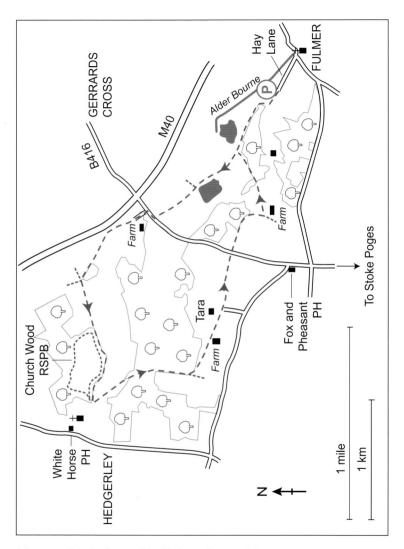

Map: use OS Explorer 172, Chiltern Society Map 24

WALK 8 ◆ FULMER

Distance 7.25 km / 4½ miles
Time 2–3 hours

Park towards end of Hay Lane, Fulmer (SU 995859) before start of private section.

Follow track past drive to Fulmer Hall then, just after entrance to Fulmer Chase, go L along valley bottom FP, following yellow arrows to B416. Go R down road, then L. At end of track, cross stile and follow edge of field, with hedge on L. After next stile, follow telegraph pole line to official entrance to Church Wood [NB: information board for optional trails round wood]. Go diagonally back L across field, up through wood and along hedge. After small footbridge and stile, turn L skirting wood, then go across field, round farm and diagonally across next field to Tara drive. Cross straight over, continuing to B416, where cross diagonally R and follow fence round to farm, then L down to valley bottom. Turn R and follow sign back to Fulmer village.

LOOK OUT FOR

April	Colt's-foot, Dog Violets, Red Dead-nettle
May	Bugle, Common Vetch, Red Campion
June	Germander Speedwell, Musk-mallow, Ribbed Melilot
July	Dark Mullein, Feverfew, Rosebay Willowherb
August	Common Mallow, Creeping Cinquefoil, Goat's-rue
September	St John's-wort, Great Willowherb, White Dead-nettle

Birds and butterflies to note may include Heron, Grey Wagtail, Woodpeckers, Coot, Moorhen; White Admiral, White-letter Hairstreak

Blackthorn 'tunnel' near Fulmer.

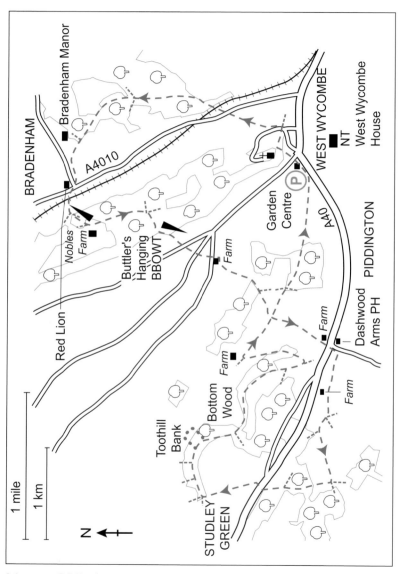

Map: use OS Explorer 171 and 172, Chiltern Society Map 7

WALK 9 ◆ WEST WYCOMBE

Distance 14.5 km / 9 miles
Time 4½–6 hours

Park in West Wycombe NT CP by
Garden Centre (SU 826948).

Cross road and climb towards
Mausoleum. At top of steps, follow
mown path R down hill, L round scrub
and R down steps to lane. Cross
diagonally R, then take L of two FPs, fork
R at arrow post, cross road and railway
and enter wood. Follow white arrows
always straight ahead, eventually
dropping to surfaced track, where L then
R round green, and L to cross main road
opposite PH. Go under railway then R to
arrow post, L up to Nobles Farm, where
turn L. At next arrow post, go R then
down through Buttler's Hangings
BBOWT Reserve, cross three roads, and
up wide track L of Chorley Farm house.
Near top of hill, follow yellow arrow
straight ahead on indistinct path,
emerging at wide gap in hedge at top
corner of field. Go R through gate then L
along fence line, down through Ham
farmyard and across main road.

Go R along BW almost to start of
copse then R along farm track to edge of
wood, where L across field, R at path
junction, following white arrows through
woods to road. Cross and go R then L
along hedge line down into Bottom
Wood. Follow wide track R along valley
bottom. [Fork L along permissive path
and L up hill to go round Toothill
Reserve.] When almost back to Ham
Farm, go L by arrow post up hill, then
follow yellow arrows between fences,
over two stiles and R along wide track,
crossing outward route. At fork, take
less-used track, veering R down sunken
way, then L almost immediately into
woods, where follow white arrows.
Emerging from trees, follow clear route
back to CP.
NB: Take great care crossing railway –
fast trains.

LOOK OUT FOR

March	Dog & Sweet Violets, Lesser Celandine
April	Cuckooflower, Field Pansy, Ground-ivy
May	Bluebell, Cowslip, Woodruff
June	Common Rock-rose, Pineappleweed, Scarlet Pimpernel
July	Hogweed, Field Bindweed, Great Willowherb
August	Traveller's-joy, Marjoram, Chiltern Gentian (R)
September	Devil's-bit Scabious, Red Bartsia, Yarrow

Birds and butterflies to note may
include Red Kite; White-letter
Hairstreak, Speckled Wood,
Meadow Brown

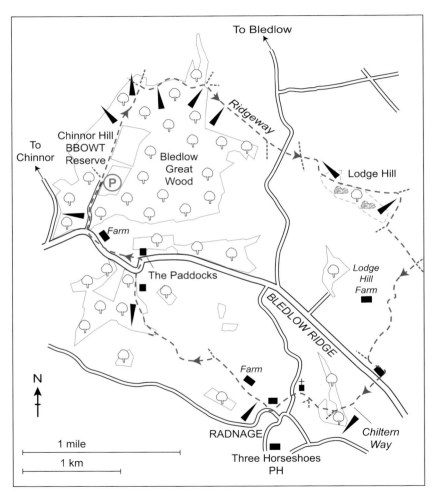

Map: use OS Explorer 171 and 181, Chiltern Society Maps 7 and 14

WALK 10 ◆ CHINNOR HILL

Distance 12 km / 7¹/₂ miles
Time 3¹/₂–4¹/₂ hours

Park at Chinnor Hill BBOWT Reserve CP at end of Hill Top Lane (SP 766002).

From CP, follow BW signed to Chinnor Barrows, passing Reserve information board. At KG L, enter Reserve and follow contour path, returning through next KG to BW which descends to junction with Ridgeway, where turn R up wood edge. On reaching open field, cross diagonally R, then follow hedge L, through KG and on to road. Continue straight across, following Ridgeway arrows up Lodge Hill and along ridge. Descend steeply, then leave Ridgeway to go R along BW. At bottom of wood, turn L on BW to join surfaced track, then R past Lodge Hill Farm, taking L fork and continuing straight ahead past small row of conifers, then R through metal KG to climb up to Bledlow Ridge. Cross straight over road and continue on Chiltern Way through wood then across fields and through churchyard to road. Take FP opposite church then R up lane, R again after Whites Farm. At fork, continue L along BW. At woods, fork R up hill to road, then R round double bend. Take FP L by The Paddocks, crossing field and through farm buildings to rejoin road. Go R for 150 m then R into Hill Top Lane and back to CP.

LOOK OUT FOR

March	Dog Violets, Dog's Mercury, Lesser Celandine
April	Common Field and Wood Speedwells, Primrose
May	Borage, Ramsons, Cow Parsley, Green Alkanet
June	Common Spotted Orchid, Common Rock-rose, Yellow Pimpernel
July	Harebell, Field Scabious, Wild Candytuft
August	Violet Helleborine, Eyebright, Carline Thistle
September	Clustered Bellflower, Common Centaury, Wild Basil

Birds and butterflies to note may include Red Kite, Nuthatch, Tree Creeper, Warblers; Brimstone, Dark Green Fritillary, Common Blue

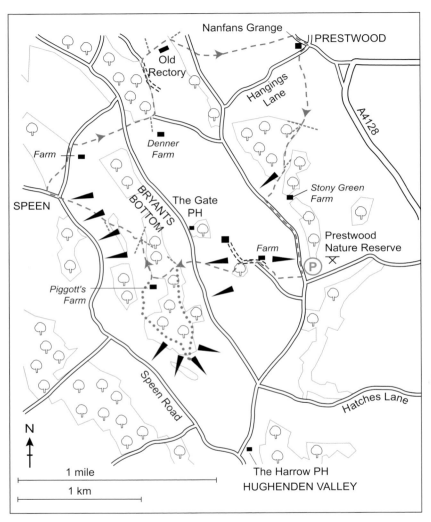

Map: use OS Explorer 172 and 181, Chiltern Society Map 12

WALK 11 ◆ PRESTWOOD

Distance 8.5 km / 5¼ miles
Time 3–4 hours

Park at Prestwood Picnic Site/Nature Reserve CP (SU 866992).

Go L along road then R up field edge. At top of hill, L over stile, R along drive, passing through gate, then 50 m down hill, L over stile in hedge, steeply down to cross valley bottom road, then up into wood. At yellow arrow post, go straight on up hill (in late April/early May, detour L around edge of wood to see Coralroot), then R along drive. At The Cottage, follow white arrow round to L, diagonally over fields into wood, where turn R, eventually dropping diagonally down to valley bottom road. Go just past Speen sign, turn R past Scout hut, then R immediately up FP through woods. At road, go L, then R diagonally across field, down and through garden to cross road and straight up other side (very steep!). At end of Denner Farm drive, go L keeping along wood edge, then L along surfaced track for c. 150 m, R past thatched cottage, and L on BW past Old Rectory. At surfaced drive, follow L for about 100 m, then L on FP, re-crossing drive and reaching valley bottom road, where cross diagonally R, and ascend on same line round copse. Follow yellow arrows on stiles, past Nanfan's Farm down drive, R at road,

R again at crossroads, and L on FP. After entering wood, fork immediately L to join surfaced track, R to road and L back to CP.
NB: Narrow lane bends for 500 m – beware occasional speedy vehicle!

LOOK OUT FOR

March	Wood Spurge, Dog Violets, Lesser Celandine
April	Coralroot, Lords-and-Ladies, Cowslip
May	Cow Parsley, Bluebell, Woodruff
June	Grass Vetchling, Bird's-foot-trefoil, Pignut
July	Common Knapweed, Common Centaury, Enchanter's-nightshade, Violet Helleborine
August	Betony, Wild Teasel, Goat's-rue, Wild Carrot
September	Devil's-bit Scabious, Eyebright (R), Autumn Gentian (R)

Birds and butterflies to note may include Red Kite, Yellowhammer, Woodpeckers, Mistle Thrush; Marbled White, Common Blue, Brimstone, Green Hairstreak

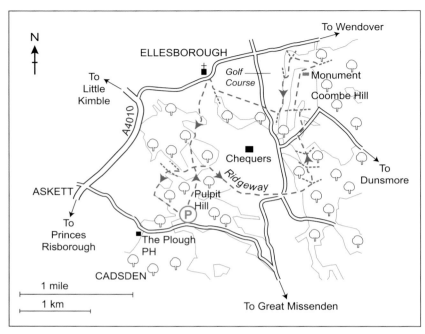

N

To Wendover

ELLESBOROUGH

Golf
Course

Monument

Coombe Hill

To
Little
Kimble

A4010

Chequers

Ridgeway

To
Dunsmore

ASKETT

Pulpit
Hill

P

To
Princes
Risborough

The Plough
PH

CADSDEN

To Great Missenden

1 mile

1 km

Map: use OS Explorer 181, Chiltern Society Map 3

Dog Violets.

WALK 12 ◆ PULPIT HILL

Distance 10 km / 6¹/₄ miles
Time 3¹/₂–4¹/₂ hours

Park at Pulpit Hill CP, Longdown Hill
(SP 833046) off A4010 at Askett.

Leave from L of CP, and go up steep hill
signed Fort. At second sign (Fort L),
continue straight ahead. Follow white
arrows on trees, crossing straight over
next track, eventually over stile at
wood edge, and R to field corner,
where join Ridgeway (Acorn symbol).
Continue R along Ridgeway, past
Chequers through woods to the
Monument, then R to sunken track.
(Continue on for 100 m to see
Gentians in September.) Turn L down
hill, taking either high or low route,
to path crossing, where L up steps
and through metal KG. Go straight
over next path and join wide track
immediately below Monument.
Continue skirting round bottom of hill
until end of golf course, where turn R,
R again along road, then L across field,
and eventually R on a track leading to
Ellesborough. Turn L along main road
past gardens, then L going diagonally
across fields to skirt round hill and
through scrub. Follow wide track
through wood. Proceed to cross
surfaced drive and go up field keeping
to fence on R, along which cross stile
and continue on other side
of fence to cross stile at top. Join
Ridgeway R all the way round Pulpit
Hill, then take BW L back to CP.

LOOK OUT FOR

March	Dog & Sweet Violets, Dog's Mercury
April	Colt's-foot, Moschatel, Wood-sorrel
May	Common Field Speedwell, Woodruff, Herb-Robert
June	Common Spotted Orchid, Wild Thyme, Viper's-bugloss
July	Nipplewort, Squinancywort, Yellow-wort
August	Dwarf Thistle, Common Knapweed, Bellflowers
September	Field Pansy, Scarlet Pimpernel, Gentians

Birds and butterflies to note may
include Red Kite; Marbled White,
Chalkhill Blue

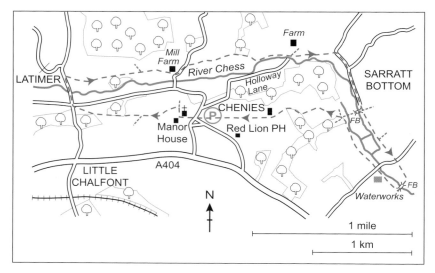

Map: use OS Explorer 172, Chiltern Society Map 5

The Chess Valley and Chenies Mill.

WALK 13 ◆ CHENIES

Distance 8.75 km / 5½ miles
Time 2½–3½ hours

Park (considerably) round or near Chenies village green (TQ 017984).

Walk up driveway towards Chenies Manor and immediately before gateway turn R on FP past Church. On entering woods, go L along wide track to wood edge, where go immediately R over stile and along top of field, then down initially fenced path to crossroads. Go straight over to edge of Latimer village, turning R through green metal gate, then KG, to follow BW along valley bottom (Chess Valley Walk). Continue through Mill Farm then L along lane. At bend, go R on FP, continuing along valley bottom and noting FB at Holloway Lane and water-cress beds on R just after. At road, bear R along Sarratt Bottom, continuing straight ahead when road goes up hill L. At end of rough track [with optional short detour R to FB], follow FP past lynchets (medieval farm terraces), crossing the lane and continuing over FB, where turn R back along the River Chess past the waterworks. Cross straight over road, and return along Chess valley until opposite distant cottages on far side of river. Here turn L over stile, then immediately R over next stile, following arrowed direction to ascend field, then L along hedge line. At wood edge, go R to skirt wood, over stile, and on to farm drive back to Chenies.

LOOK OUT FOR

April	White Dead-nettle, Bluebell, Marsh-marigold
May	Common Vetch, Cuckooflower, Green Alkanet
June	Chalkstream Water-crowfoot, Common Mallow, Ragged-Robin
July	Meadowsweet, Common Ragwort, Red Bartsia
August	Common Centaury, Purple-loosestrife, Willowherbs
September	Himalayan Balsam, Yarrow, Hogweed

Birds to note may include Coot, Moorhen, Heron

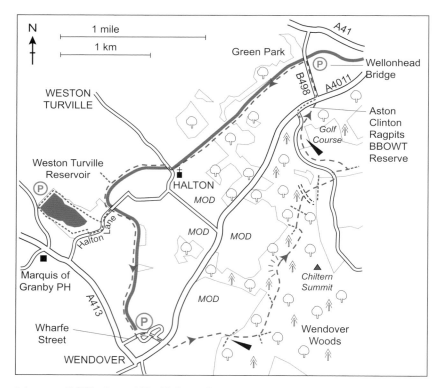

Map: use OS Explorer 183, Chiltern Society Map 18

WALK 14 ◆ WENDOVER

Distance 10 km / 6¹/₄ miles
Time 3¹/₂–4¹/₂ hours

Park on Wharfe Street at end of
Wendover Canal (SP 869082).

Walk E along Manor Road, cross
A4011, then straight up Colet Road,
L into Barlow Road, and straight up
Beechwood Lane. At entrance to
Wendover Woods, go straight up hill,
taking second L at yellow arrow post
near summit, then L past Fitness Trail
information board to follow wide track.
At fork, keep R passing viewpoint and
sunken track crossing. At post showing
cycle track 'To main road', continue
down for 200 m then R up wall-edged
path, over forest road, eventually
leaving woods and crossing field past
trig point to road. Cross diagonally L
and pass mountain biking CP; then
sharp L to descend steeply through
woods and round golf course by white
posts to A4011. [Detour to Aston
Clinton Ragpits BBOWT Reserve (R):
L along main road, L up side road, L
again into woods by small lay-by.
Follow Badger sign to BBOWT board.]
Cross and go down Stablebridge Road,
B489, turning R through canal CP,
then L along canal. Follow canal
towpath, crossing to other side at
village of Halton. [Detour to Weston
Turville Reservoir: At next bridge, go
R along Halton Lane, turn R by bend

LOOK OUT FOR	
March	Dog's Mercury, Sweet Violet, Lesser Celandine
April	Lords-and-Ladies, Garlic Mustard, Dog Violets
May	Herb-Robert, Common Milkwort (R), Cow Parsley
June	Yellow Iris, Greater Butterfly Orchid (R), Fragrant Orchid (R)
July	Himalayan Balsam, Field Scabious (R), Pyramidal Orchid (R)
August	Marjoram, Willowherbs, Autumn Gentian (R)
September	Yarrow, Eyebright (R), Harebell

Birds and butterflies to note may
include Heron, Grey Wagtail,
Mallard, Moorhen, Coot;
Chalkhill Blue, Duke of Burgundy
Fritillary, Peacock

in road, through KG into wood, then
L to follow path anti-clockwise round
reservoir and back on to Halton Lane.
Retrace steps back to canal.] Continue
along towpath back to start.

Opposite: Fragrant Orchids and Common Twayblades at Aston Clinton Ragpits BBOWT Reserve.

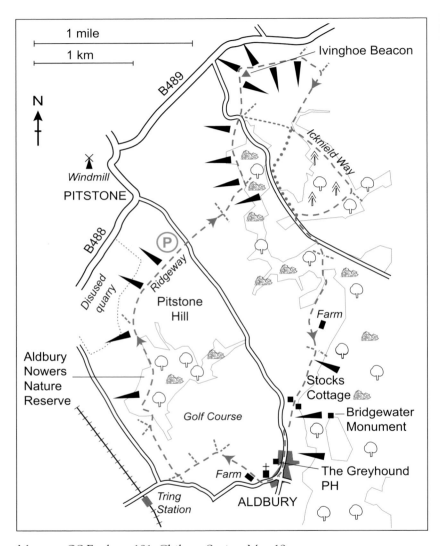

Map: use OS Explorer 181, Chiltern Society Map 19

WALK 15 ◆ PITSTONE HILL

Distance 13.5 km / 8½ miles
Time 4½–5½ hours

Park in NT CP, Pitstone Hill
(SP 955149).

Cross road and follow Ridgeway (Acorn
symbol) to cross next road [Shortcut: R
on Icknield Way along field boundary]
then straight over to top of Ivinghoe
Beacon (start/finish of Ridgeway). Bear
R along ridge (Whipsnade Lion visible
on distant hillside). As path descends
gradually towards stile in fence, turn R
down to field gate then bear R across
field to join Icknield Way. [Shortcut:
Follow wide track up hill then FP parallel
with road.] Turn L into wood and
continue to clearing on L, where R for
20 m then L up wide track to road. Turn
L on R-hand verge path for 320 m, then
enter woods on NT BW parallel to road,
veering R to join yellow arrowed FP.
Continue down slope to bottom of dip,
straight up other side and over stile at
edge of wood. Follow path round field
margin, then across 3 fields, cross BW
and follow fence, then waymarks to
village of Aldbury. Walk through village,
bearing R after the pond, past the
church, then R along FP round farm.
Here join narrow path past barn
(Hertfordshire Way). Continue up to golf
course (noting Bridgewater Monument
to R above trees), where turn L,
continuing straight ahead until rejoining
Ridgeway. Turn R and continue past
Aldbury Nowers Nature Reserve, up
Pitstone Hill and back to CP.

LOOK OUT FOR

April	Cowslip, Field Pansy, Greater Stitchwort
May	Field Madder, Ramsons, Sanicle
June	Fairy Flax, Hoary Plantain, Yellow-rattle
July	Common Valerian, Musk Thistle, Spiny Restharrow
August	Carline Thistle, Hedge Parsley, Wild Carrot
September	Devil's-bit Scabious, Harebell, White Dead-nettle

Birds and butterflies to note may
include Meadow Pipit, Kestrel,
Buzzard, Skylark; Marbled White,
Duke of Burgundy Fritillary, Small
Blue, Brown Argus

Beech trees.

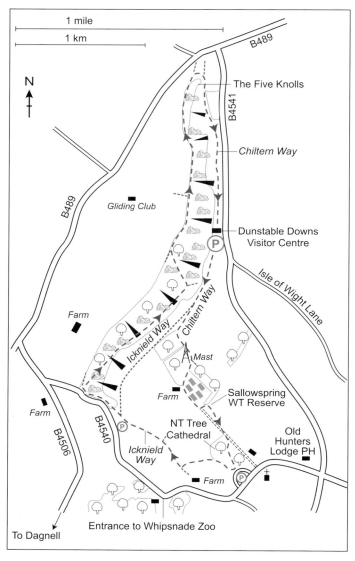

Map: use OS Explorer 181, Chiltern Society Map 21

WALK 16 • DUNSTABLE DOWNS

Distance 7.25 km / 4½ miles
Time 2¼–3½ hours

Park at Dunstable Downs Visitor Centre CP on the B4541 (TL 008198).

Follow direction of fingerpost at entrance to CP and cross open area to join Chiltern Way, then follow arrow discs. Continue across surfaced track, forking R at phone mast to pass Sallowspring estate. Immediately after estate, take FP L into Sallowspring Reserve, follow around perimeter back on to road, then FP R into Whipsnade NT area. Leave Chiltern Way to explore NT Tree Cathedral [information board in hedge at centre of site], exiting W back on to Chiltern Way. Skirt Dell Farm animal enclosures, then R on Icknield Way back to Downs. Drop down after CP on L, keeping parallel with road. On reaching road, turn R along bottom of Downs through L-hand KG. After second KG turn R then L and follow sunken track up slope and along contour. At metal farm gate, go L steeply down to bottom FP where R through KG, immediately fork R, and continue along boundary FP. Eventually go through KG and along back of gardens to open grassy area, where R up hill past Five Knolls, and follow Chiltern Way back to Visitor Centre. NB: Two very steep downward slopes. The Downs are an Open Access area so it is possible to explore off-path.

LOOK OUT FOR

April	Cowslip, Greater Stitchwort, Ground-ivy
May	Germander Speedwell, Salad Burnet, Yellow Archangel
June	Bush Vetch, Common Spotted Orchid, Common Twayblade
July	Meadow Vetchling, Squinancywort, Yellow-wort
August	Scentless Mayweed, Eyebright, Red Bartsia
September	Agrimony, Chiltern Gentian, Common Toadflax

Butterflies to note may include Chalkhill Blue, Duke of Burgundy Fritillary, Small Tortoiseshell

Greater Knapweed, Scabious and Wild Carrot near Dunstable Downs.

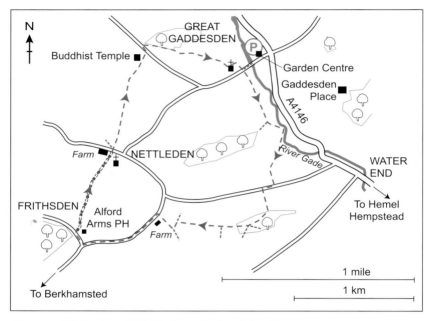

Map: use OS Explorer 182, Chiltern Society Map 20

River Gade in July.

WALK 17 ◆ GADDESDEN

Distance 6 km / 3³/₄ miles
Time 2–3 hours

Park at Garden Centre, Great
Gaddesden (TL 031114), just off the
A4146 from Hemel Hempstead.

Walk R over bridge (noting plants in
and around river to R of bridge), L on
to permissive path, going between
River Gade and pond, through flood
meadow and exiting by metal farm
gate. [If this area is closed because of
flooding, use public FP running along
W edge.] Continue ahead between
river and another pond, crossing FB,
then going diagonally R across field
to road. Go R for 50 m, then L up into
woods. At path junction (marker post),
fork R and follow less distinct path to
lower corner of wood. Having admired
the view of Gaddesden Place beyond
the Gade, go straight across field,
turning L at boundary fence, then R
down side of farm to main road, where
go L for 500 m, then R to Frithsden.
Immediately after Alford Arms PH,
turn R up steep lane which then
descends under old carriage bridge to
Nettleden. Turn L after Roman Farm
to end of village, and then R up FP to
St Margaret's (Buddhist Centre). Go
L along lane, then R down wood edge
and diagonally across fields to Great
Gaddesden church. Pass through
churchyard, then R to road and L
back to start.

LOOK OUT FOR

April	Lesser Celandine, Red Dead-nettle, White Dead-nettle
May	Brooklime, Cuckooflower, Goat's-beard
June	Fumitory, Water-cress, White Bryony
July	Field Bindweed, Meadowsweet, Musk-mallow
August	Red Bartsia, Scentless Mayweed, Great Willowherb
September	Perennial Sow-thistle, Yarrow, Himalayan Balsam

Birds to note may include
Kingfisher, Skylark, Coot, Mallard

NB: Main road to Frithsden can be
busy. For maximum visibility, L side of
road recommended until after bend,
then safer to cross to R side.

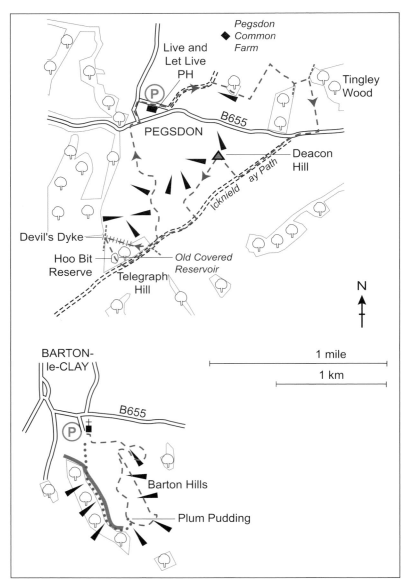

Map: use OS Explorer 193, Chiltern Society Maps 25 (BH) and 26 (P)

WALK 18 • PEGSDON & BARTON HILLS

A: Pegsdon (P)
Distance 6.5 km / 4 miles
Time 2–3 hours

Park in Pegsdon (TL 119303).

Pass Live and Let Live PH then follow
Chiltern Way sign L along road towards
Pegsdon Common Farm. Take first R up
hill, L along field edge, R up track, then
L to edge of Tingley Wood where R.
At B655 go R for 250 m, then L along
Icknield Way. Cross stile by information
board to ascend Deacon Hill, then L
along ridge to hedge, where L to rejoin
Icknield Way. Look R for metal field gate
after KG, where branch R down past
Devil's Dyke. At path junction turn
immediately L, coming back up through
wood and SE corner of Hoo Bit Reserve,
to Icknield Way by covered reservoir.
Continue L back to KG on L, through
which bear R and through next KG on
to Reserve. Follow contour R passing first
ridge, then L down next ridge. At valley
bottom, go up path opposite and out of
Reserve R, back to start.

B: Barton Hills (BH)
Distance 2.5 km / 1¹/₂ miles
Time 1–2 hours

Park in Church Lane, Barton-le-Clay
(TL 085304).

At end of lane, L on Chiltern Way BW.
Ignore Reserve gate and follow BW up
hill, entering Reserve through next KG
on R. Walk round old quarry area, then
along flat FP to where steps join from
R. Continue up steps through second
KG (*) signed Chiltern Way. Follow
fence line to top of 'Plum Pudding',
then descend along its ridge and drop
down, either to source of stream, and
continue back through woods, or return
along same side at lower level, just
above scrub line but climbing to exit
by same KG as above (*), down all
steps and through KG back to church.

LOOK OUT FOR

April	Pasque Flower (BH), Moschatel, Sweet & Hairy Violets
May	Hound's-tongue, Star-of-Bethlehem, Cowslip
June	Common Valerian (BH), Wild Candytuft (P), Dropwort (BH)
July	Lady's Bedstraw, Pignut, Selfheal
August	Devil's-bit Scabious (BH), Autumn Gentian, Fluellens
September	Clustered Bellflower, Yarrow, Harebell

Birds to note may include Skylark, Lapwing, Kestrel

FURTHER READING

Allen, D. E. and G. Hatfield, *Medicinal Plants in Folk Tradition: An Ethnobotany of Britain and Ireland* (Timber Press, 2004)

Berkshire, Buckinghamshire and Oxfordshire Wildlife Trust (BBOWT), *Where 2 Go 4 Wildlife* (BBOWT, 2004)

Blamey, M., R. Fitter and A. Fitter, *Wild Flowers of Britain and Ireland* (A. & C. Black, 2003)

Blamey, M. and C. Grey-Wilson, *Illustrated Flora of Britain and Northern Europe* (Hodder & Stoughton, 1994)

Blunt, W., *The Complete Naturalist* (Collins, 1971)

Bown, D., *RHS Encyclopedia of Herbs* (Dorling Kindersley, 1995)

Chevallier, A., *The Encyclopedia of Medicinal Plants* (Dorling Kindersley, 1996)

Coombes, A. J., *Dictionary of Plant Names* (Collingridge, 1985)

Culpeper, N., *Culpeper's Complete Herbal* (1652; reprint Wordsworth, 1995)

Davison, M. W. (ed.), *Field Guide to the Wild Flowers of Britain* (Reader's Digest, 1995)

English Nature, *Chilterns Natural Area Profile* (English Nature, 1997)

Fitter, R. (ed.), *The Wildlife of the Thames Counties* (Robert Dugdale/BBONT, 1985)

Fortey, R., *The Hidden Landscape: Journey into the Geological Past* (Jonathan Cape, 1993)

Gerard, J., *Gerard's Herbal* (1597; reprint Senate, 1994)

Gilmour, J. and M. Walters, *Wild Flowers* (Collins New Naturalist Series, 1954)

Gledhill, D., *The Names of Plants* (Cambridge University Press, 2002)

Grigson, G., *Dictionary of English Plant Names* (Lane, 1973)

Harrap, A. and S. Harrap, *Orchids of Britain and Ireland: A Field and Site Guide* (A. & C. Black, 2005)

Hepple, L. W. and A. M. Doggett, *The Chilterns* (Phillimore, 1994, 2nd edition)

Louseley, J. E., *Wild Flowers of Chalk and Limestone* (Collins New Naturalist Series, 1950)

Mabey, R., *Flora Britannica* (Sinclair-Stevenson, 1996)

Morris, J. K., *History in Chiltern Woods* (Chiltern Woodlands Project, 1999)

Press, B. and Gibbons, B., *Wild Flowers of Britain and Europe – Photographic Field Guide* (New Holland, 1993)

Rackham, O., *The History of the Countryside* (Phoenix, 1997)

Stace, C., *New Flora of the British Isles* (Cambridge University Press, 1997)

Vickery, R., *A Dictionary of Plant Lore* (Oxford University Press, 1995)

INDEX OF PLANT NAMES

This index covers plants in the Directory and the Walks of this volume.

Agrimony (*Agrimonia eupatoria*) 32, 129, 151

Alkanet, Green (*Pentaglottis sempervirens*) 104, 139, 145

Anemone, Wood (*Anemone nemorosa*) 49, 123, 129, 131, 133

Angelica, Wild (*Angelica sylvestris*) 49, 121, 129

Archangel, Yellow (*Lamiastrum galeobdolon*) 32, 127, 131, 151

Avens, Wood (*Geum urbanum*) 33, 123

Balsam, Himalayan (*Impatiens glandulifera*) 89, 121, 145, 147, 153

Balsam, Orange (*Impatiens capensis*) 102, 125

Bartsia, Red (*Odontites vernus*) 89, 123, 137, 145, 151, 153

Basil, Wild (*Clinopodium vulgare*) 70, 133, 139

Bedstraw, Hedge (*Galium mollugo*) 50, 125

Bedstraw, Lady's (*Galium verum*) 33, 155

Bellflower, Clustered (*Campanula glomerata*) 104, 125, 127, 139, 143, 155

Bellflower, Nettle-leaved (*Campanula trachelium*) 105, 123, 129, 143

Betony (*Stachys officinalis*) 70, 129, 141

Bindweed, Field (*Convolvulus arvensis*) 50, 137, 153

Bird's-foot-trefoil, Common (*Lotus corniculatus*) 34, 141

Bittersweet (*Solanum dulcamara*) 71, 133

Bluebell (*Hyacinthoides non-scripta*) 105, 125, 129, 137, 141, 145

Borage (*Borago officinalis*) 106, 139

Brooklime (*Veronica beccabunga*) 106, 153

Bryony, White (*Bryonia dioica*) 51, 153

Bugle (*Ajuga reptans*) 107, 131, 135

Burnet, Salad (*Sanguisorba minor*) 102, 127, 151

Campion, Bladder (*Silene vulgaris*) 51, 121

Campion, Red (*Silene dioica*) 90, 135

Campion, White (*Silene latifolia*) 52, 125

Candytuft, Wild (*Iberis amara*) 52, 127, 139, 155

Carrot, Wild (*Daucus carota*) 53, 141, 149

Catmint, Wild (*Nepeta cataria*) 53, 133

Celandine, Lesser (*Ranunculus ficaria*) 34, 123, 131, 137, 139, 141, 147, 153

Centaury, Common (*Centaurium erythraea*) 90, 131, 139, 141, 145

Chicory (*Cichorium intybus*) 107, 129

Cinquefoil, Creeping (*Potentilla reptans*) 35, 133, 135

Colt's-foot (*Tussilago farfara*) 35, 125, 135, 143

Comfrey, Common (*Symphytum officinale*) 71, 121, 125

Coralroot (*Cardamine bulbifera*) 91, 141

Cowslip (*Primula veris*) 36, 127, 137, 141, 149, 151, 155

Crane's-bill, Cut-leaved (*Geranium dissectum*) 91, 125

Crane's-bill, Dove's-foot (*Geranium molle*) 92, 123

Crane's-bill, Hedgerow (*Geranium pyrenaicum*) 92, 121

Cuckooflower (*Cardamine pratensis*) 93, 121, 137, 145, 153

Dead-nettle, Red (*Lamium purpureum*) 72, 121, 135, 153

Dead-nettle, White (*Lamium album*) 54, 123, 133, 135, 145, 149, 153

Dropwort (*Filipendula vulgaris*) 54, 127, 155

Enchanter's-nightshade (*Circaea lutetiana*) 55, 125, 141
Eyebright (*Euphrasia* spp.) 55, 127, 131, 139, 141, 147, 151

Feverfew (*Tanacetum parthenium*) 56, 135
Flax, Fairy (*Linum catharticum*) 56, 149
Fleabane, Common (*Pulicaria dysenterica*) 36, 125
Fluellen, Round-leaved (*Kickxia spuria*) 37, 129, 155
Fluellen, Sharp-leaved (*Kickxia elatine*), 37, 129, 155
Fumitory (*Fumaria officinalis*) 93, 153

Gentian, Autumn (*Gentianella amarella*) 72, 125, 127, 131, 141, 143, 147, 155
Gentian, Chiltern (*Gentianella germanica*) 73, 127, 131, 137, 143, 151
Goat's-beard (*Tragopogon pratensis*) 37, 153
Goat's-rue (*Galega officinalis*) 73, 135, 141
Ground-ivy (*Glechoma hederacea*) 74, 125, 129, 133, 137, 151

Harebell (*Campanula rotundifolia*) 108, 131, 139, 147, 149, 155
Helleborine, Violet (*Epipactis purpurata*) 112, 139, 141
Hemlock (*Conium maculatum*) 57, 125
Hemp-agrimony (*Eupatorium cannabinum*) 94, 121, 133
Herb Bennet see Avens, Wood
Herb-Robert (*Geranium robertianum*) 94, 123, 143, 147
Hogweed (*Heracleum sphondylium*) 57, 137, 145
Horehound, Black (*Ballota nigra*) 74, 121
Hound's-tongue (*Cynoglossum officinale*) 75, 155

Iris, Stinking (*Iris foetidissima*) 75, 133
Iris, Yellow (*Iris pseudacorus*) 38, 147

Knapweed, Common (*Centaurea nigra*) 76, 141, 143
Knapweed, Greater (*Centaurea scabiosa*) 76, 125, 131

Lords-and-Ladies (*Arum maculatum*) 112, 141, 147
Lucerne (*Medicago sativa*) 77, 129

Madder, Field (*Sherardia arvensis*) 77, 125, 149
Mallow, Common (*Malva sylvestris*) 95, 135, 145
Marjoram (*Origanum vulgare*) 78, 131, 137, 147
Marsh-marigold (*Caltha palustris*) 38, 145
Mayweed, Scentless (*Tripleurospermum inodorum*) 58, 133, 151, 153
Meadowsweet (*Filipendula ulmaria*) 58, 145, 153
Melilot, Ribbed (*Melilotus officinalis*) 39, 135
Melilot, White (*Melilotus albus*) 39
Mercury, Dog's (*Mercurialis perennis*) 113, 125, 143, 147
Mignonette, Wild (*Reseda lutea*) 39, 123
Milkwort, Chalk (*Polygala calcarea*) 108
Milkwort, Common (*Polygala vulgaris*) 108, 127, 147
Mint, Water (*Mentha aquatica*) 78
Moschatel (*Adoxa moschatellina*) 113, 123, 143, 155
Mullein, Dark (*Verbascum nigrum*) 40, 127, 135
Musk-mallow (*Malva moschata*) 95, 135, 153
Mustard, Garlic (*Alliaria petiolata*) 59, 121, 131, 147

Nipplewort (*Lapsana communis*) 40, 143

Orchid, Bee (*Ophrys apifera*) 96, 123, 127

Orchid, Common Spotted (*Dactylorhiza fuchsii*) 79, 139, 143, 151

Orchid, Fragrant (*Gymnadenia conopsea*) 96, 147

Orchid, Frog (*Coeloglossum viride*) 114, 127

Orchid, Greater Butterfly (*Platanthera chlorantha*) 59, 127, 147

Orchid, Lady (*Orchis purpurea*) 97, 125

Orchid, Military (*Orchis militaris*) 97, 133

Orchid, Monkey (*Orchis simia*) 98, 125

Orchid, Pyramidal (*Anacamptis pyramidalis*) 98, 131, 147

Orchid, Southern Marsh (*Dactylorhiza praetermissa*) 79, 129

Pansy, Field (*Viola arvensis*) 60, 121, 137, 143, 149

Parsley, Cow (*Anthriscus sylvestris*) 60, 139, 141, 147

Parsley, Fool's (*Aethusa cynapium*) 61, 123

Parsley, Hedge (*Torilis japonica*) 61, 149

Parsnip, Wild (*Pastinaca sativa*) 41, 125, 131

Pasque Flower (*Pulsatilla vulgaris*) 80, 155

Pignut (*Conopodium majus*) 62, 141, 155

Pimpernel, Scarlet (*Anagallis arvensis*) 103, 129, 131, 137, 143

Pimpernel, Yellow (*Lysimachia nemorum*) 41, 133, 139

Pineappleweed (*Matricaria discoidea*) 42, 137

Plantain, Hoary (*Plantago media*) 114, 149

Ploughman's-spikenard (*Inula conyzae*) 42, 127, 133

Primrose (*Primula vulgaris*) 43, 129, 133, 139

Purple-loosestrife (*Lythrum salicaria*) 80, 121, 125, 145

Ragged-Robin (*Lychnis flos-cuculi*) 99, 145

Ragwort, Common (*Senecio jacobaea*) 43, 145

Ramsons (*Allium ursinum*) 62, 131, 139, 149

Restharrow, Common (*Ononis repens*) 99

Restharrow, Spiny (*Ononis spinosa*) 99, 149

Rock-rose, Common (*Helianthemum nummularium*) 44, 137, 139

St John's-wort, Perforate (*Hypericum perforatum*) 44, 131, 135

Sanicle (*Sanicula europaea*) 63, 149

Scabious, Devil's-bit (*Succisa pratensis*) 81, 123, 137, 141, 149, 155

Scabious, Field (*Knautia arvensis*) 81, 139, 147

Selfheal (*Prunella vulgaris*) 82, 133, 155

Silverweed (*Potentilla anserina*) 45, 133

Sneezewort (*Achillea ptarmica*) 63, 121, 129

Snowdrop (*Galanthus nivalis*) 123

Snowflake, Summer (*Leucojum aestivum*) 64, 121, 125

Sow-thistle, Perennial (*Sonchus arvensis*) 45, 121, 153

Speedwell, Common Field (*Veronica persica*) 109, 121, 123, 139, 143

Speedwell, Germander (*Veronica chamaedrys*) 109, 123, 135, 151

Speedwell, Ivy-leaved (*Veronica hederifolia*) 110, 121

Speedwell, Thyme-leaved (*Veronica serpyllifolia*) 110, 133

Speedwell, Wood (*Veronica montana*) 111, 139

Spurge, Wood (*Euphorbia amygdaloides*) 115, 127, 131, 133, 141

Squinancywort (*Asperula cynanchica*) 64, 143, 151

Star-of-Bethlehem (*Ornithogalum angustifolium*) 65, 155

Stitchwort, Greater (*Stellaria holostea*)
65, 131, 149, 151
Stitchwort, Lesser (*Stellaria graminea*)
65
Strawberry, Wild (*Fragaria vesca*) 66,
133

Teasel, Wild (*Dipsacus fullonum*) 82,
141
Thistle, Carline (*Carlina vulgaris*) 46,
127, 139, 149
Thistle, Dwarf (*Cirsium acaule*) 83, 123,
143
Thistle, Musk (*Carduus nutans*) 83,
127, 149
Thyme, Wild (*Thymus polytrichus*) 84,
143
Toadflax, Common (*Linaria vulgaris*)
46, 125, 127, 129, 151
Toadflax, Pale (*Linaria repens*) 84, 125,
129, 131
Tormentil (*Potentilla erecta*) 47, 129
Traveller's-joy (*Clematis vitalba*) 66, 137
Twayblade, Common (*Listera ovata*)
115, 151

Valerian, Common (*Valeriana
officinalis*) 100, 149, 155
Vervain (*Verbena officinalis*) 85, 131
Vetch, Bush (*Vicia sepium*) 85, 151
Vetch, Common (*Vicia sativa*) 86, 121,
135, 145
Vetch, Tufted (*Vicia cracca*) 86, 121
Vetchling, Grass (*Lathyrus nissolia*) 103,
141
Vetchling, Meadow (*Lathyrus pratensis*)
47, 151
Violet, Common Dog (*Viola riviniana*)
87, 123, 125, 127, 133, 135, 137,
139, 141, 143, 147
Violet, Early Dog (*Viola
reichenbachiana*) 87, 125, 127, 133,
135, 137, 139, 141, 143, 147
Violet, Hairy (*Viola hirta*) 87, 155

Violet, Sweet (*Viola odorata*) 87, 123,
131, 147, 155
Viper's-bugloss (*Echium vulgare*) 111, 143

Water-cress (*Rorippa nasturtium-
aquaticum*) 67, 153
Water-crowfoot, Chalkstream
(*Ranunculus penicillatus*) 67, 145
Water-crowfoot, River (*Ranunculus
fluitans*) 67
Water-dropwort, Hemlock (*Oenanthe
crocata*) 68, 121
Willowherb, Great (*Epilobium hirsutum*)
100, 135, 137, 145, 147, 153
Willowherb, Rosebay (*Chamerion
angustifolium*) 101, 135, 145, 147
Woodruff (*Galium odoratum*) 68, 129,
137, 141, 143
Wood-sorrel (*Oxalis acetosella*) 69, 129,
131, 133, 143
Woundwort, Hedge (*Stachys sylvatica*) 88,
123
Woundwort, Marsh (*Stachys palustris*) 88,
121

Yarrow (*Achillea millefolium*) 69, 123,
133, 137, 145, 147, 153, 155
Yellow-rattle (*Rhinanthus minor*) 48, 149
Yellow-wort (*Blackstonia perfoliata*) 48,
123, 143, 151